ENOUGH LOVE

ESSAYS OF RESILIENCE AND TRIUMPH
FROM A FEMALE ROMANIAN
AIR FORCE PILOT

BY
RODIKA PONICI

ENOUGH LOVE LLC

Enough Love
Copyright ©2021 by Rodika Ponici
All rights reserved.

ISBN: 978-1-7378829-1-6

No part of this book may be used or reproduced in any manner whatsoever without written permission except in the case of brief quotations embodied in critical articles and reviews.

Printed in USA

For My Adi

CONTENTS

FOREWORD Fall Seven Times, Stand Up Eight   7

1	Childhood Is a Promise That Is Never Kept	9
2	Knowledge Is Power	25
3	Opposites Attract	35
4	Love Is a Sunny Place	41
5	Don't Judge a Book by Its Cover	53
6	Where There's a Will, There's a Way	63
7	There's a First Time for Everything	79
8	No Day So Clear but Hath Dark Clouds	83
9	Home Is Where the Heart Is	89
10	The Heart Wants What It Wants	97
11	Every Day Is a New Beginning	103
12	No Gain Without Pain	109
13	All's Fair in Love and War	117
14	Where There Is Life, There Is Hope	125
15	A Woman's Place Is in the Kitchen	137
16	A Journey of a Thousand Miles Begins with a Single Step	143
17	Hope for the Best, Prepare for the Worst	153
18	Nature Will Have Its Course	163
19	Two Shorten the Road	167
20	All's Well That Ends Well	181
21	Grief Divided Is Made Lighter	193
22	Every Cloud Has a Silver Lining	203
23	Better Late Than Never	211
24	Love Lasts a Lifetime	217

FOREWORD

FALL SEVEN TIMES, STAND UP EIGHT

Resilience is the courage to start all over again, the pain of leaving everything that you ever had and believed in behind, the craziness to leave the comfort for the unknown and the willingness to break through.

Drive is the passion to embrace a new life at high speeds to make up for lost time, to catch up with it like you never left or never came, and to not have the luxury to slow down or catch your breath.

Dedication is finding the balance between not changing yourself, your beliefs, and your values, but still fitting in and finding acceptance.

Struggle is learning to speak and think again when you already thought that you knew enough to get you through life.

Patience is waiting for better times, the power to get where you want to be, and feel comfortable—back to where you were once—and on the way there to not get embarrassed or feel sorry for yourself, but to enjoy every moment of your journey.

Self-assurance is knowing when to slow down and pace yourself and not doubting that you'll get there. *Will I ever catch on? Will my life just be running?*

Ambition is reaching for the stars to find out how far you can stretch and where your limits are, doing your best to get there without trying to be a perfectionist.

Bravery is taking risks and not getting scared when you take one step forward and two steps back, and having hopes for the day when you'll take two forward and one back.

Courage is living up to expectations and having the strength to always fight for what you think is right and worthy, but realizing when it's the end of the battle or time to move on.

Wisdom is the acceptance that you do not always have to be brave; it's okay to ask for help or cry and still not view yourself as weak.

Understanding is surviving the pitfalls, embracing the failures, and getting up again to continue; being able to trust people again, and over again, and to give each one of them a fair chance.

Compassion is making a difference in people's lives, bringing out the best in them, seeing them smile, trying to make them happy and not asking anything in return; searching for treasures and valuing them when you find them.

Our lives have a path all figured out, but we stray from our path and need to find it again. The search takes years of resilience, drive, dedication, struggle, patience, and self-assurance, and in the end we look back and do not see the break in the path and say to ourselves that it has been a worthy run…with no regrets. We are content with ourselves and happy because we have lived our lives with ambition, bravery, courage, wisdom, understanding, and compassion. And if there will come a day when we'll lose the path again—we find the determination and willpower to start from the beginning—again.

I

CHILDHOOD IS A PROMISE THAT IS NEVER KEPT

My first images as a child took place when I was a year and a half old and being lifted into the air. You wouldn't think a person could remember a moment of their life at only eighteen months of age, yet my memory of that day is as strong and secure in my mind as the hands that lifted me to safety.

That summer of 1968 we were visiting my mom's family in a charming little clay house, with a tiny veranda to match, in the remote village of Teioasa. In my first memory, I wore a blue knit sweater that did little to combat the fever that plagued me. In the sun I felt as if my blood boiled under my skin. In the shade I shook with uncontrollable chills. My parents and I embarked on the long walk from the village to reach the bus stop, and from there to travel to the nearest hospital.

My legs felt leaden as we trekked along a shortcut through neighbors' gardens. I remember the flowers in incandescent yellows and shocking pinks under the bright Romanian sun. When the gardens ended and the forest began, I looked at the long curvaceous path before me, winding endlessly through the trees, and felt I could go no farther. That's when arms reached down and lifted me up, a moment that's never left my mind. Was it my father, seeing my exhaustion and carrying me the rest of the way? Or my mother's arms coming to my rescue?

At the hospital, a lady in a starched and stiff white coat made a grand entrance into the room. I instantly and inwardly retreated.

She administered injections, and I remember cringing and turning away from the needles, not understanding how receiving a shot would take away my unbearable pain. I just wanted to go back to the little clay house, curl up on the hearth, and drift into my dreams.

* * *

Vasile, my father, knew that Aglaia, with her chestnut hair and blue sky eyes, was the woman he wanted to marry. She'd grown up in Teioasa with nine brothers and sisters, spending much of her life at that point helping to raise her younger siblings and stepsiblings. Her mother died when she was very young, leaving her father with five small children to care for. He remarried a woman who had a daughter, and the two would go on to have another four children of their own. Though all ten children got along well together, it was not always easy for my mother to look after them. Left alone all day while their parents were at work, they found various forms of mischief, including taking pillows up to the attic and then jumping down to ground level with the hopes that the pillows would break their fall. It worked…sometimes.

My mother was fifteen when she met my father, who was a few years older and serving his time in the army, far away from the village in which he'd grown up. He had dark eyes and a commanding presence, only heightened by his uniform. Vasile was known for his relaxed and easy manner, always on display when he would dance with other girls. With Aglaia, however, it was different. He'd call on her at home, standing straight and formal at her door, hoping that in time Aglaia's father would give his blessing for the two to wed.

It would be Vasile's own mother, my grandmother Firoanda, who had something to say about his wishes. When he told his mother of his plans to wed the fifteen-year-old, she would have none of it. My grandmother was shy of five feet tall, but a woman of fierce determination, something you wouldn't expect from a tiny woman already worn out from raising six children on her own. Her husband, my grandfather, had died when their children were still very young. She never remarried; perhaps her ferocity was borne of necessity.

"You will marry who I tell you to marry," Firoanda demanded, but her attempts to arrange a marriage for her son were no match for teenage love. Vasile and Aglaia wed against her wishes and had four children, of which I was the second. My parents didn't have much say when it came to their family planning. In an effort to boost the population of Romania, Communist President Nicolae Ceaușescu issued a decree outlawing any form of contraception and abortion for women unless they had already given birth to four children.

When I was little, my parents tended cows for a living. Their work was a thirty-minute walk from home, where they milked and cared for the animals. I remember walking the dirt road to visit them during the day and, when my mother wasn't looking, licking the salt lick, unperturbed by the fact that I shared it with the bovine creatures.

For most of our days, my three brothers and I were locked inside of our home, as my parents saw little other choice. Nelu, a year and three months older than me, was my ally. We were bonded in our plight of having to care for our younger brothers. Doru was four years younger and had the bluest of eyes. Marius was the baby of the family and he wailed with abandon when our parents would leave in the morning. Eventually Doru would begin crying too, perhaps as a show of solidarity, and Nelu and I would roll our eyes in unison.

"Hey, Rodica," Nelu whispered one morning as the little ones finally eased from all out crying to mere sniffling. "I have an idea. Let's escape through the window."

The boredom of being locked in our tiny home all day, every

day, was giving us cabin fever.

"What if Mom and Dad find out?" I asked, weighing the idea of freedom against the likely eventuality of punishment.

"They won't find out," he assured me. "We'll come back before they get home from work."

It took both of us lifting the heavy, wooden-framed glass to pry up the window.

As soon as Nelu and I touched down outside, two-year-old Doru and one-year-old Marius began crying again. Nelu and I looked at each other, and then at the two pairs of hands reaching up to the window from inside the house, pleading to come with us.

"What do you think, Rodica?" Nelu asked.

"We should leave them inside," I answered. "They'll be safe at home."

We spent the day breathing in the freedom of fresh air, wandering through the street and along the canal, finding other children to play with in the hot summer sun. In the afternoon, as we sat on the banks and threw stones into the water, Doru came wandering up to us.

"What are you doing here?" Nelu asked. "You were supposed to stay at home."

"They must have managed to climb out the window after us," I said.

"Doru, where's Marius?" Nelu asked, but Doru simply looked around as if suddenly remembering that he had a little brother who might be trailing behind.

"He's probably still at home," I said. "We'd better get back." I took Doru's hand and the three of us walked back home, only to find it empty.

"Marius?" I called. "Where's Marius?"

Nelu and Doru echoed my calls, but our youngest brother was nowhere to be found. We made our way back to the canal in case he'd climbed out the window and gone looking for us, but still, no Marius.

"Oh no, what if he fell into the canal?" My heart raced.

"Rodica," Nelu said, "we have to get back to the house now. We have to get back before Mom and Dad return from work. Let's go and maybe we'll find Marius along the way."

We rushed back home, Doru's hand in mine and his little legs struggling to keep up. I scanned the water and banks of the canal, wanting to set eyes on Marius but also terrified of where and in what condition I might find him.

"I'm sure he'll come home, Rodica. Let's just get back inside."

As we scrambled back to climb through the window, we saw that we were too late. Our parents were walking up the dusty road to our home, Marius in between them, holding our mother's hand.

I wanted to relax in relief, but saw my mother's face contorted with anger as they got closer. She looked as if a storm raged beneath her skin. Her eyes bored into mine, only mine. She released Marius and tightly grabbed my forearm.

"Why did you do that?" she demanded. *"Why did you leave and put your little brothers in danger? Why didn't you take better care of them?"*

She screamed these questions at me and I said nothing, simply looked back at her in fear, my eyes and mouth wide in paralysis. At six years old, I felt not only her anger, but also the difficulty of being trapped in the space between child and caretaker. While she depended on me to be a babysitter, Nelu and I were still children ourselves. She raised her other arm and I shut my eyes tight, tensed my muscles waiting for a blow to land.

"We need to feed the chickens now," my father intervened, gently pulling my mother back and standing in between us. "Come everyone, it's time for chores."

✷ ✷ ✷

After first grade, we moved from the tiny village of Barmod to the city of Salonta, famous throughout Romania for its sausage, "Salam de Sibiu Salonta." Fittingly, my father began working at the sausage factory. Not long after the move (and perhaps also because it was not long after misplacing my youngest brother) I was sent to a small village called Burda at the base of the Carpathian mountains to live with my grandmother Firoanda, who had long since made peace with the fact that her son married someone not of her choosing. At least their union yielded children, and of her grandchildren, I was the favorite. Looking back, I can only guess that the years I spent living with my grandmother were meant to ease my parents' situation. And if my grandmother was going to take in one of her grandchildren, it was going to be me, perhaps because I was the only girl.

I spent many hours climbing the cherry tree next to my grandmother's house, which was tall enough that, from its highest branches, I could reach the roof of the house, where I'd gorge on fruit, and pine for my family. Nelu's absence in my daily life felt like a pinprick in my heart as I pictured him wrangling Doru and Marius, trying to keep them out of trouble. He was the other half of my soul and I missed him terribly.

My grandmother would come out of the house and find me on the roof. Shocked and in disbelief, she would quietly tell my uncle Teodore to try to bring me down. On my way to gobble on cherries, I never thought about how I'd get back down.

My uncle Teodore lived in the house with grandmother and me, though he must have been in his thirties by then and most of his other siblings had since moved away. Teodore was slight and worn from a life of labor, but handsome just the same, and kind. Teodore was deaf, used lots of hand gestures to communicate when he spoke, and I knew to always turn my head to face him when I talked because he depended on reading lips.

"Uncle," I once asked with the brazenness of a child, "why

aren't you married?"

He looked wistful, contemplative, as if choosing his words. Before he could speak, Grandmother answered for him. "There was a girl he liked, but he has no business getting married. After all, he can't even hear anything." Teodore traced circles on the floor with his foot and, almost imperceptibly, shook his head in disagreement.

Grandmother had one of her other sons in the village, my uncle Gheorghe. Firoanda and Gheorghe didn't speak, as she was still angry that he'd married a girl of his own choosing and not one she would have picked for him. Though she'd reconciled with my father for the same transgression, she hadn't yet forgiven Gheorghe, despite the fact that he lived across the street from her.

Gheorghe's home was special in our village, as he owned the only television. He'd been determined to own one and had worked hard to do so. Villagers packed his living room every Saturday for an hour of comedy with Laurel and Hardy. I'd spend the whole week looking forward to the ten minutes of *Tom & Jerry* that played every Sunday at one in the afternoon. Those ten minutes were far more entertaining than the dull and boring Romanian cartoons that played for a few minutes in the evenings. Though I was a conscientious and obedient child, I was also bold enough to sneak visits to Gheorghe's home to watch television and play with my cousins.

* * *

"Are you excited to go see your parents and brothers?" Teodore asked.

"Yes," I answered, "but I'll miss you and Grandmother." And, I thought, *Tom & Jerry*. I was delighted to find upon returning home that my parents had since bought a television too. There would be no need to miss my pals *Tom & Jerry*.

Cartoons aside, I was thrilled to be able to go home and visit with my family, especially Nelu, for a weekend. I'd missed them profoundly since moving in with Grandmother. At the same time, I'd grown extremely close to my grandmother, clinging to her in the absence of my home.

During my weekend visit at home, I realized that I'd become a foreigner. My brothers had to make room for me to sleep; my mother would always forget to set out six plates instead of five. These were little daggers to my heart and my confidence, making me feel like a stranger to that house, intruding into new routines and habits with which I was unfamiliar. Though it was good to see my parents and brothers, Nelu in particular, I spent most of my time counting down the minutes until I could return to Grandmother. When the time came, I burst into Grandmother's home ready to throw my arms around her, but she wasn't there.

"Where is Grandmother?" I asked Teodore.

"She went to the church."

I desperately wanted to see Grandmother and let her know I'd returned. My heart couldn't wait another second. But the Communist government made it clear that visiting the churches was forbidden. The older generation got away with it, but a child in a church was unacceptable. I reasoned that it would only be for a second, I'd just run in quickly and let her know I'd returned and then run out again. What harm could it do?

I raced to the small Greek Orthodox church near the center of our village and felt a wave of relief wash over me when I saw Grandmother. I hugged her tightly and told her how much I'd missed her, before she shooed me out the door so that I wouldn't get in trouble.

The next day at school, I lowered my head when a classmate announced that I'd been spotted entering the church. Tears burned at the corners of my eyes as the teacher informed me I'd be held after class for a two-hour detention. I was not a child who got in trouble and to be seen as anything other than studious and diligent filled me with feelings of failure.

As a child, my studiousness went hand in hand with patriotism. At the age of nine I walked over ten miles to the next town, Beius, to see the Communist president, Nicolae Ceaușescu. The Communist Party had directed area schools to have children lined up along the roads, cheering as the president's motorcade passed. Spirits were high and as the car passed, carrying the president and his wife, my eyes filled with tears and I felt a fluttering in my stomach. I had just seen the president and his wife! I was naïve to the miseries that my government subjected its people to. It would be much later in life when my patriotism would give way to the disappointment of reality.

* * *

At the age of ten, I returned to Salonta to live with my parents and brothers. For the next three years Nelu would be not only my brother, but also my protector and best friend. While our parents busied themselves with work and the endless task of providing for themselves and the four of us, there was little time left for teaching us the ways of the world or talking about the future. They knew that school would be instrumental in our lives, but both of our parents had only the opportunity to attend school through the fourth grade, so they lacked the basic foundation of how to support us and encourage us. But Nelu and I shared a love of dreaming beyond the borders of our home. Nelu was disciplined and dedicated, qualities I was committed to emulating. He was also exceedingly brave.

"We could sneak up to the border," Nelu suggested one day when we were visiting our maternal grandmother. "Maybe we'll see some soldiers there."

"I don't want to go to the border," I said quickly. Grandmother had told us many times of the dogs that patrolled the stretch of land where Romania ended and the Soviet territory began its insatiable expanse of land. She warned of military hounds who could smell little children and, I imagined, eat them.

"You scared?" Nelu asked.

"Of course not." I lifted my chin and set my shoulders back. My fears competed with my desire to mirror Nelu's bravery. "But I think Grandmother's 'mamaliga' polenta should be ready by now, so we should get back."

My favorite part of visiting my mother's mother was her heavenly polenta. Every day she made a giant round of polenta for us to eat in lieu of bread. She'd stir it slowly in a great pot over the fire, then pour it in a pan to set when it was cooked. Before we'd eat, she'd put the polenta on a plate, slide a string underneath, and then pull the string up to cut through the polenta. I always marvelled at her precision, and by the time she was through, the circle would have been perfectly cut into ten equal slices.

Nothing went to waste, so after she'd prepared the polenta, she'd pour milk in the giant pot and scrape down the sides of it to get any morsels that remained. To this day, the taste of that milk and polenta remains both heavily and heavenly in my memories.

Second only to polenta was my love of oranges. Like most children, we pined throughout the year for Christmas, when the government doled out small plastic bags for fathers to give to their children. Each plastic bag held a few sweets and one orange. I'd think of that orange throughout the whole year and try to savor it when that magical day finally came. To this day, I cannot think of Christmas without thinking of oranges.

The oven was the centerpiece of Grandmother's home. A massive clay structure that occupied most of the living room and which we used for both cooking and heating, the oven rose four feet into the air. With a belly full of polenta, I'd climb the five steps built into the side of the oven to the bed on top where we children slept. Warmth radiated up through my small sleeping pad where I'd snuggle in among blankets and pillows. Though already a child, I'd sleep like a baby.

* * *

When Nelu was accepted into one of Romania's three military high schools, highly competitive institutions, I suffered a mix of pride and sorrow. On one hand, I was ecstatic that Nelu was escaping the slim prospects of our small town of Salonta. At fourteen he was leaving home to embark on a journey toward a better life. Both Nelu and I were well aware that the competitive military high school could serve as a gateway to possibilities we hadn't yet even imagined. It might mean the difference between a career and a life of manual labor, or exposure to the bustle of modern cities versus the quiet drone of remote rural life.

On the other hand, I was crushed. My bond with my brother was the spark of motivation that kept me going, that kept me dreaming. The prospect of life without my constant companion, whom I'd known since birth, who knew me better than anyone else alive, was bleak. Nelu was my rock and when he left, I felt my soul begin to wither. The responsibility of our younger brothers now sat fully on my shoulders. The one person who I felt truly understood me was being stripped from my daily life.

"I'll come back to visit, Rodica," he said on the day he left. "Don't worry, I'll be back on breaks and holidays."

"I know," I said, trying to muster a smile for his benefit. I wiped at my eyes. "I know." I vowed that when he returned for the Christmas break, I'd share my orange with him.

* * *

"Before we build our house, Rodica, we have to make a small house for us to stay in during construction," my father explained.

"Where will our tiny house be?" I asked.

"Right here," he said, gesturing to a small patch of yard next to our garden. "It will be just big enough to house us while I tear down our old house so that I can rebuild it. Just wait and see. It will be a dream house!"

With a lot of muscle, the tiny house began to take shape over the next few months. A single room served as kitchen, living room, and bedroom, while we continued to use an outhouse for the bathroom. Though space was tight, we were happy in the tiny house.

"Let's see who can find me first," my father would shout, initiating a game of hide-and-seek in the tiny house, much to the delight of Doru and Marius. Even I would struggle to find him, and I was always amazed at his creativity in finding new places to hide in such a small space.

He can't be in the cabinet, I'd think. *It would be impossible to fit in there.* But after searching every other conceivable nook, we'd open the cabinet to find that he'd somehow contorted his body to make it fit.

Doru and Marius would scream and giggle when they found him.

"You found me!" father would shout. "And now I'm going to get you!" He'd chase the boys as they ran gleefully around him in circles.

When they began building our house, my parents were united by the project. They worked as a team to fulfill their shared dream. Somewhere along the way, however, their dreams and paths began to diverge. The unity they'd once shared in their marriage dissipated. The happy memories of those days soon gave way to darker ones. My father's progress on rebuilding our house slowed, while his drinking picked up pace. He and my mother began to laugh less and argue more.

"I'm going to finish the house," my father announced routinely as the months, then years ticked by.

Mother rolled her eyes. "Yes, we know, Vasile. At least, that's what you keep saying."

"Truly, Aglaia, I'm going to finish it and we'll have a bathroom and the children will have their own rooms and it's going to be the best house in town. You'll see."

My father had always been a dreamer, but his progress toward that dream was sporadic at best. He'd set to work on the construction plans that had been marinating in his mind, but then let his efforts dwindle over time. Though I wasn't as dismissive as my mother, I sometimes had my doubts, but at other times allowed a kernel of excitement to form inside of me, and I longed for the day when my father's masterpiece would be finished.

One night, my brothers, mother and I all slept when suddenly the light switched on overhead. Blinded by the searing light, we squinted to see what was going on. My father stumbled near the light switch.

"Why did you turn on the light?" my mother yelled. "Everyone was sleeping!"

"My dear kids," my father slurred. "My dear kids, what else can I do for you? I'll build you a house with your own rooms, but what else can I do for my dear kids?" he rambled.

"You've come home drunk again, Vasile," mother hissed. "You're just a drunk."

My father's demeanor switched like the light he'd just turned on, sudden and blinding. He swung his arm through the air, backhanding my mother in the face. She stumbled to the floor and he began smacking the side of her head. Doru and Marius cried and hid under their shared blanket.

"Stop!" I yelled. "Please stop. Don't hurt Mom!" As he swung his arm back to deliver another blow, I grabbed on to keep it from landing. My hand caught his as it moved forward and suddenly I heard and felt a sickening crack in my father's finger.

My mother scrambled to her feet and ran to put a hand on Doru and Marius, still whimpering under their blanket. Father stood in what looked a mix of shock and amusement, holding his hand in front of his face and staring at his index finger, which now bent away from his hand at an unnatural angle.

Though the broken finger would inhibit my father's ability to work, he never showed any anger toward me for it. Despite my parents' spiralling marriage and my father's escalating drinking, he was always tender with us children. I knew, unquestioningly, that I was always in his heart.

✳ ✳ ✳

By middle school, it was time for me to start contributing by earning money in the fields during the summer break. My mother would send me off at six in the morning with a small sandwich to one of the locations in the village where the bus would come. Many of my friends had the same summer duties. It was a forty-minute bus ride to work the government's fields, picking beans or tomatoes under the hot summer sun. We'd return home exhausted in the evenings, then wake early the next morning to do it all over again.

On the occasional day off, I'd escape the tension of home and the responsibility of caring for Doru and Marius by visiting my mom's sister, whom we called "Nani" and who often helped us and loved us like her own children. Other times I'd meet up with my friends at the canal. I didn't know how to swim, but on one July afternoon mustered up the courage to try to swim across, like my friends were. As soon as I jumped in the water, I felt a force pulling me quickly under, my body became a useless and sinking ragdoll. I remember the feel of a foreign hand grasping onto my arm and pulling me out. One of my friends had the quick thinking to save me and once again, just as when I'd been a feverish toddler, I was grateful for the hands that came reaching down from above. Though we continued to gather at the canal when we could, that was the first and last time I attempted swimming in it.

On our way home from the canal, we'd often sneak over the

fence into the government's cherry orchard. We knew that it was prohibited, but those cherries numbered in the thousands, deep red and juicy. We'd stuff ourselves with them as quickly as possible, before the orchard guard would see us and start yelling. He'd pick up a big stick to imply that if he managed to reach us, he was going to make sure we got a good whack. That was always enough to send us scurrying home.

✳ ✳ ✳

We moved into my father's dream house when it was far from finished. It was just two rooms and a kitchen, but my father loved to talk about one day finishing it. There would be stairs leading to more rooms, a bathroom, a garage despite the fact that we never owned a car, and stucco. "All for my children," he'd say, usually after coming home from a bar, "it's all for you." As he drank more, both in quantity and frequency, progress on the house ground to a halt.

2

KNOWLEDGE IS POWER

"We are going on a trip to Oradea. I need volunteers. Who is coming?" our gym teacher asked. A wide smile spread across his face, while both his voice and body language exuded energy. It was infectious and my hand instantly shot into the air.

As a sophomore in high school, I hadn't yet been on many trips away from our small town. The school trips often cost money that my parents simply didn't have, but by asking for volunteers, our teacher had made it clear that this particular trip was paid for by the school. My opportunity to see a new city had just presented itself. Little did I know that there was much more in store for me.

As the train rattled away from the station, I realized that none of us had any idea where we were going or what might occur, but we didn't care. The disruption to our normal day was welcomed by all. Before we knew it, the train was slowing into a station and we were herded from there to a subway. The next leg of our journey ended in a part of town filled with military units. When we finally reached our destination, we found ourselves in a sunny field among countless other students, boys and girls all of similar ages in our early teenage years.

Murmurs rippled through the crowd, wonderings of what we were doing there and what was to come. I hoped we'd get to see the town, I was always eager to catch a glimpse of new places and learn what might be out there in the world. Minutes dragged into hours and our hopefulness dissipated. We were hungry and hot, and went from wondering what would happen to just hoping we'd soon be able to leave. Impatience enfolded my body and mind as I began to view the entire trip as senseless. Then a voice began calling out names and they came to mine.

"Corha, Rodica" a woman shouted. I stepped forward with the others who had been called. When the group of us had been assembled, we were led into a shooting range and a cold, metal rifle was thrust into my hands. There was no instruction or talk of safety, I was simply handed a gun and told to shoot at a target, as if the act was as commonplace as tying one's shoes.

In time I'd learn the three positions of shooting, from the ground, from one knee, and standing up, which proved to be the most difficult. As I stood there, feeling chills from the cold metal and struggling to support the weapon with shaking arms, I didn't know why I was being asked to do such a thing. I was barely fifteen years of age, but I was also obedient and diligent. Having grown up in a Communist society where you are told what to do, as well as how to feel about it, I simply did what I was told.

The woman who'd handed me the rifle smiled encouragingly as I took aim at a paper target with circles on it. No one told me how to breathe, or that the rhythm of your breath is timed with the pull of the trigger. When I first fired the weapon I was shocked at the recoil of the gun against my shoulder. The woman with the warm eyes smiled again, encouraging me to go ahead with the next bullet. And I did. Again and again, one by one, until I'd exhausted the clip.

When I was finished, I was happy to return to the yard under the bright sun with my fellow students. I was ready to leave. To my surprise, we weren't preparing to return home. Excruciating hours passed by, during which I thought I might faint from lack of food.

"Corha, Rodica!" My name was called again just as I thought I might fall asleep on my feet. I was led back into the shooting range and told to repeat the exercise. What was the point of it all?

Everything I felt went against my excitement of that morning, when our teacher had first asked for volunteers and I thought we were headed for a field trip to a new city.

"You did really well the first time," the smiling lady said. "Your grouping was impressive. You'll need to concentrate to do well again." I noticed that while before there had been other students also firing, I was now the only one. She gave me fifty more rounds to fire, fifty cold, repulsive bullets. I did as I was told. Relief washed over me after the final shot, along with a fresh wave of confusion, exhaustion, and hunger.

A group of adults huddled around my paper target, analyzing my results. My legs ached from a day of standing. After an interminable amount of time, the smiling woman turned to me and said, "You may now wait back outside with the others. Don't leave yet."

I wasn't the only student there wrestling with confusion. Hundreds of girls and boys were put through this same test with little explanation, but we knew better than to ask too many questions. We did as we were told, never questioning those in charge.

Eventually, a man emerged into the yard and the students' murmurs fell to a hush. He called out a name and the student stepped forward accepting a third place certificate. Another name was announced and a tall, wiry boy emerged from the crowd to accept his second place certificate.

"And first place," the man announced, "is Corha, Rodica."

I was stunned, not only to learn that I'd won first place, but also that what had taken place had been a contest. Emotional and overwhelmed, I stepped forward to accept my prize. After doing so, the warm-eyed woman found me again and said only, "You will be contacted soon." By whom or for what purpose, I didn't know, nor did I care. I was simply happy to move on from that place, hopefully to see the city and get something to eat.

* * *

My father's health had been declining. His breathing grew more labored and ragged, and it became commonplace for him to have multiple stays in the hospital throughout the year. And so it came to be that when the head of the military shooting club came to town, to convince my parents to let me attend the military club in Oradea, we all trekked to the hospital where my father would participate in the conversation from his hospital bed.

"She'll get lost in a big city," he protested. "I don't think she should go."

"There are many other girls her age there," the man countered. "She'll attend high school, eat in the canteen, and live in the military hotel. It is a good opportunity, as long as she agrees to continued participation and practice in the shooting club."

I steadied myself despite my spinning head and the butterflies swirling in my stomach. I knew that these opportunities were rare, that they'd spotted enough natural talent in my shooting abilities which was now somehow opening up new doors for me. *Please say yes*, I thought, wringing my hands by my father's bedside.

In the week that followed I begged my father for his permission, both silently and overtly. When he finally agreed, I could tell that he was happy for me, but also apprehensive about my future and how I would fare beyond the reach of his love and protection.

Two weeks after getting my father's permission, I found myself in an entirely new world. A different city, new school, and life away from home. I thought of Nelu during those early days, wondering if he'd had similar experiences, excitement, and fears.

My excruciating schedule began immediately. I spent six days in classes and the evenings in military club training. The weekend (which was only Sunday) was equally gruelling, but spent entirely on military training. Downtime was nonexistent. I felt overwhelmed and tired, but did my best to keep up, though the toll it was taking on me was undeniable.

One Saturday as I dragged myself to training, I realized that I was both feverish and pale. I could hardly hold my gun in my arms and I struggled to focus on the target. Voices drifting behind me barely registered.

"What's wrong with her?" The training coach's friend was speaking. He was a balding, beer-bellied man who would often hang around the training site.

The coach responded, "She must have had a rough night, if you know what I mean." I glanced back in time to see him wink at his friend.

I didn't know what they meant, not really. My head pounded. It took all of my strength to lift my gun and aim at the target. After firing my rounds, I turned to find my coach's friend standing behind me, his eyes shining with a mischief that made me uncomfortable. He used his body to block my path, making it difficult for me to get around him. For the rest of practice, I felt his eyes burrowing into my skin. It was as if his gaze was eating me alive. I felt crushed by the weight of it and the fever raging through my body. Both were inescapable.

The next morning, on Sunday, I struggled to get out of bed. While trying to drag myself to the bathroom, I collapsed in the hallway. *Why is my body giving up on me*, I wondered. *What will the coach say?* I was not the sort of person to let down my coach. I worried about missing training and what my coach would say. Participation was mandatory under all circumstances, but my limbs were made of lead. When I opened my eyes again, with no knowledge of how long I'd been unconscious, my coach, who was a tough man to please, was standing over me.

"Can you hear me, Rodica?" he asked. I tried to nod but wasn't sure if my head actually moved. He put his hand on my forehead. "I need to get you to the hospital."

For the next two weeks I recuperated from pneumonia at a

quarantined hospital. I was not allowed visitors, even my parents, so I stayed utterly alone in the hospital bed, wishing that Nelu could be there to talk with me, wondering how he was filling his days. The pain of loneliness during that time was equal to the pain that ripped through my body.

When I healed physically, I was permitted to return to the dorm and school and practice, but my joy at being out of solitary confinement was short-lived. There was my coach's friend, leering at me every day of practice. His eyes followed my every move and it felt as if his stare burned my skin. I did my best to keep my head down and stay out of his way, but it was no use. He followed me and harassed me constantly. One day, he handed me a letter.

Though he was my coach's friend and not someone in a specific position of authority over me, he was still an adult. Being handed a letter felt serious, important, as if I'd done something wrong or there was some cause for an official document. It would turn out to be nothing of the sort. I was embarrassed when he handed me the letter at the end of training one day, but obediently took it, put it in my pocket, and returned to my dormitory.

The confusion I felt from the words he'd written cannot be overstated. On the one hand, I didn't know what some of it meant, he used terminology that my naïve, fifteen-year-old mind couldn't comprehend. On the other hand, I had a crystal clear sense of what he was getting at, that the letter was his harassment elevated to a new level, putting in words the descriptions of various sex acts he wanted to perform upon me. I felt like helpless prey and knew that as a young female student, the best I could hope for was to stay away from this man. I could not tell my coach or parents or confess to my fellow students. Speaking of such things would likely make matters worse. On top of an innate shyness, I was also living in a society which didn't acknowledge the existence of harassment.

After the letter, I wanted to fold in upon myself. I felt physically ill whenever I saw the man, as now his leering had been compounded by putting into words what was going through his mind. I felt a deep sense of shame and a searing distrust of the adults around me. Weren't they there to guide me and teach me, as opposed to prey upon young students to appease themselves sexually? In disappointment and depression, I longed for a way out of my situation, where I'd no longer have to occupy the same room as this vile man.

My way out came because of academics. As I was in tenth grade, I was preparing to take the exams to move on to eleventh grade. This is an instrumental point in Romanian education, an important exam that decides a student's ability to continue with eleventh and twelfth grades and then on to college. With my rigorous training schedule with the military shooting club, I was left no time to study. When I asked my coach for more time, he said no. In his mind, the best course of action for me was to simply attend a local two-year college so that I could continue in the club, as opposed to aiming for a more ambitious institution. Though I was appreciative of what the military club had provided me, I also felt that the opportunities had run their course; I wanted to set my sights on something more. I wanted to follow my own dream and attend a good college.

Just as I'd begged my father to let me leave Salonta for Oradea, now I found myself begging him to allow me to return. When he relented, I removed myself from the military shooting club, but still had to inform my head teacher of my plans. He'd been difficult to read throughout my time there, a stern man who always left you wondering where you stood with him. I'd had to work hard to keep up with his advanced math lessons, but with dedication had been able to do so. When I told him of my plans to return to Salonta, he suddenly looked concerned, more emotion than I'd seen him display all semester.

"Why?" he quietly asked.

"I need time to study for the exams, but I can't do that if I'm in the military shooting club," I explained. "There is so much time spent training. But if I'm not in the military shooting club, then I can't afford the tuition and room and board. All of that is paid for, but only if I'm in the club."

I knew that asking my parents for money was out of the question. They already worked hard to make ends meet and I couldn't place that burden on them.

The teacher opened up to me in a way I hadn't thought possible. He told me of programs and housing for students who couldn't afford to pay. He urged me to find a way to stay.

"You'll get lost in Salonta," he said. "You have huge potential. Please try to stay."

It saddened me that it wasn't until that moment that I realized how much my teacher truly cared about me and felt invested in my education. I've always appreciated the time he took to speak with me, to let me know that I was right to set my sights high, even if I couldn't end up staying in his class, which turned out to be the case.

When I left Oradea to return home, I worried about how my friends would treat me upon my return, if they might belittle me for leaving in the first place, but they welcomed me with open arms. But rather than spend my newfound freedom with my friends, I buckled down and studied in earnest. The work paid off and I went on to receive some of the highest marks on my exams. I had not only myself to thank for my achievements, but the teacher in Oradea who pushed me, encouraged me, and, ultimately, believed in me.

* * *

In Salonta I once again found myself caring for Doru and Marius, despite the fact that they were well older than I had been when I'd cared for them as babies. I'd often have to coax them from playing in a nearby field to get them to do their homework.

Doru was relatively quiet and, for the most part, tried to stay out of trouble. Marius, however, was still a handful, and now a puzzle on top of that. I'd yell at him every time I'd catch him with a cigarette. He'd spend a mere thirty minutes on homework that should have taken him two hours. When I'd demand to see his work, it would miraculously be both complete and correct. My little brothers were no longer little, but I never was able to make them understand how much work I'd done to help our parents when I was their age, and marvelled at their ability to get out of all the tasks with which I'd been laden.

In addition to my studies and my little brothers, I tended to our garden where our father had planted roses. In time I added annuals and perennials. I loved watching the blooms flourish under my care, the feel of working the soil. Above all, I enjoyed the simplicity of playing with water, of feeling the wet pavement of the walkway beneath my feet.

My mother by then had a washing machine, so I'd water the plants and then take my bucket to the neighborhood fountain, fill it with water, and bring it back to fill our washing machine. When it was done, I'd hang the clothes on a line to dry. I have fond memories of working side by side with my mother's sister, Aunt Nani. Years before, when we were little, my mother's siblings had traveled from the other side of the country to help out. Over the years, they'd married and moved away, one by one, but Nani was always close by and quick to lend a hand. Her kindness made a lasting impression on me. I have equally fond memories of relatives on my father's side. I loved my Uncle Lazar, though he moved far away with his family and we were rarely able to see him. And though we didn't often see my Aunt Floarea, a strong woman with a big heart, she was always there when we truly needed her.

When I longed for an escape, I'd dive into the pages of a book, lose myself in the tales of Alexandre Dumas and dream of d'Artagnan's bravery. I felt, in a sense, rescued by literature. At the same time, I wondered if my journey wasn't destined to someday lead me to become a rescuer myself.

3
OPPOSITES ATTRACT

On Christmas Eve, as giant snowflakes fell peacefully from the sky, our home bustled with excitement. Not only were we preparing for the holidays, but also to celebrate Nelu's eighteenth birthday. When I heard the door open behind me, I assumed it was my mother back from shopping. I wanted to make sure she'd remembered the butter, but when I turned around, I found myself face to face with a stranger.

I blushed. Not because I found him particularly handsome or felt an instant attraction, but because unexpectedly we were suddenly nose to nose. Adrian, who went by Adi, was one of Nelu's classmates from the military high school, coming to stay for a few days to celebrate my brother's birthday. At least that's what I thought. I later learned that Adi had seen a picture of me and said to Nelu, "You have a beautiful sister and I want to meet her. I know you didn't invite me to your birthday, but I'm coming anyway. I'll be at the train station. And if you don't pick me up, I'll find out where you live and come anyway." Nelu wasn't sure if his friend was serious, but sure enough when he went to the train station, there was Adi.

Rather than enticing, I found Adi's nearness to me off-putting, as well as the fact that he didn't even acknowledge my mother when she entered and stood just a few feet away from me. He'd spend the rest of the day following me around, as if he wanted to help, but also with an air of arrogance about him that I didn't care for. He'd ask me how I felt about school, then put down the education system, which was what I saw as my means of escape to a better life. It seemed to me that he was criticizing my dreams.

I didn't notice whether or not Adi was attractive, that is until my neighbor stopped by, asking if Adi was already paired up. During times of celebration and dancing, the teenagers would pair up with a partner. There was nothing romantic about pairing up and it had nothing to do with flirting or crushes, but was a system we used to make sure that everyone had a dance partner and no one would be left out. My neighbor, having caught a glimpse of Adi, desperately wanted to know if he was available. Her desire to be paired with him didn't bother me, not necessarily because I'd already been paired up with another of Nelu's classmates, but because in my mind Adi wasn't worth a second look. My neighbor's question caused me to look at Adi in a different way. Was there something I was missing about my brother's confident friend? Something I hadn't seen before?

My neighbor was ecstatic to learn that Adi hadn't yet been paired up and I told her she could have him. Then I turned my attention to the party. I would be busy in the role of hostess and ensuring that my brother's 18th birthday was properly celebrated. Nelu had a blast and a highlight of the evening was when he asked me to dance. My brother and I were an undeniably awesome pair on the dance floor. We loved to dance and easily floated across the room, following one another without words. As Nelu and I twirled, I caught glimpses of Adi and could feel his eyes on me.

The boys were on winter break and Adi was staying with us for two nights before he'd return to his own home. By the end of that night, the crowd had dwindled down, though my girlfriend was still there, wanting to spend as much time with Adi as she could. At one point as I walked by where they sat on the couch, Adi reached out and grabbed me, pulling me down next to him and kissing me. I felt awkward as my girlfriend, who obviously liked him, sat on the other side of him. I slapped him and went to stand back up, but he pulled me down again. In total, he pulled me down three times, kissed me three times, and received a slap in return three times before I got up and angrily told him to mind the lady he was with. Though I didn't like the attention Adi was showing me, I was also growing more comfortable around him and began to see that what I'd initially thought of as arrogance was oftentimes just his way of playfulness and expressing his confidence.

The next day Nelu and his friends went to see a movie. My girlfriend and I were going to see the same movie at a later time. When we arrived, the boys were leaving.

"You guys went to the movie without us and now we'll have to walk home alone and it's getting dark," I said. "Which one of you is going to watch it again so you can walk us home after?"

Nelu and his friends looked down at the ground, not wanting to make eye contact and admit that they didn't want to stay for a second showing. There was one exception, as Adi looked me in the eye and without hesitation said, "I will."

"Thank you, Adi," I said. I appreciated his gesture, though I didn't appreciate, during the movie, when he tried to put his hand on my leg.

When it was time for Nelu and his friends to leave, Adi told my brother that he wanted to come back in a week's time to celebrate the New Year, but only if he would be paired up with me. Nelu told me this, but also warned me. Though Adi was one of Nelu's closest friends, he also saw him as someone who could never be serious about a relationship. I learned then that this was why Adi had never visited our home before, despite the fact that Nelu had visited Adi's home many times. Nelu was, after all, still my older brother and my protector. He didn't want to see me get hurt and for this reason had kept distance between Adi and his baby sister. He knew that I was young and naïve, and feared I might get my heart broken. All the same, Nelu agreed to invite Adi back for the New Year if I wanted him to.

I said yes, which changed my life forever.

* * *

By the time New Year's rolled around, I was curious about Adi. Who was this charming, sarcastic guy? Why was he interested in me? I'd given him no encouragement and had made it clear that my priorities were in my education and helping out my family.

Before long it seemed that whenever there was a task before me, there was also Adi with a bright smile and ready to help. Whether it was household chores or pushing the small water cart a mile to get drinking water, there was Adi. I grew to look forward to his help and his company.

On the morning of New Year's Eve I reached for a jar of peppers and cabbage.

"Here, let me help you," Adi jumped in.

"Do you like pickled peppers stuffed with cabbage?" I asked.

"Yes," he replied. "It's one of my favorites."

"I'm not sure I believe you," I said.

"What if I told you I love you," Adi said, "would you believe me then?"

I felt the heat of a blush rise through my face and knew that yes, if Adi said those words to me, I would believe him. I answered, "Yes." My heart was both young and credulous. Time would tell if his love was true. Incidentally, I later learned that Adi did not like peppers and cabbage at all.

The party that evening took place at a friend's home across the road. Adi and I danced all evening, and I floated across the room in his arms, losing myself in his eyes. How had I ever thought him arrogant? It was clear that he was merely confident, and he had an enviable positivity about him. Nothing brought him down. It was as if his smile was his strength, and by remaining upbeat he could rise above the most difficult of situations.

We danced for hours to songs in English. We couldn't understand the lyrics, but the melodies were romantic and as we glided across the room, I knew we were falling in love. My heart felt light and full all at once.

At midnight the calendar turned to January 1, which celebrated Saint Vasile, so we rushed back across the street to wish my dad, named Vasile, many more years. It was a family tradition. I will never experience a New Year without thinking of my father.

After visiting my father, neither Adi nor I were ready to return to the party. Without words, we mutually acknowledged the desire to stroll together along the outskirts of town. My arm linked through his, I felt the heat of his body in contrast to the chill of the winter air. We found a bench and sat down to talk as snow began to fall. Our conversations flowed effortlessly and we knew that there was no other place in the world that either of us needed to be in that moment, other than sitting on that bench together in the early hours of the new year. Being together made sense in a way that I'll never be able to fully articulate. In those moments, I felt that all was right with the world.

We lost track of time and when we finally returned home to the party where our friends were still having fun, I could see that Nelu had been waiting in worry. When he saw that I was okay, relief washed over his face. When he saw that I was not only okay, but also happy, he broke into a smile himself. Something in that moment convinced Nelu that he didn't need to worry about me and Adi, and he never again worried about Adi's intentions with me.

Love is shameless. It makes you feel liberated of worries, poverty or hardships. You see the world from a new perspective, almost like you can confront it head on with all your inner power and strength. You are filled with an immense force of tangling and unifying energy, and nothing can take you down.

Until I met Adi I felt embarrassed talking to guys, embarrassed about my home situation, my dad's drinking, our house in a perpetual state of construction, the mud in the backyard. Everything seemed a mess of poverty. But with Adi I felt on top of the world, nothing could have gone wrong, there was no embarrassment, just joy. I was able to hold my head high. He'd seen my family and where I lived, had even stayed with us. He saw only who I truly was and nothing else about my situation mattered, not the unfinished house or the broken fence or my father drinking or my parents constantly arguing. That was the power of love.

I later asked Adi why Nelu had the impression that he was never serious about girls. He answered, "I just hadn't met the right girl." He followed this with, "You know, one day you are going to marry me." Though part of me wanted to believe him, another part of me was scared. I tried my hardest many times *not* to believe him, but in time he proved worthy of both my trust and love.

4
LOVE IS A SUNNY PLACE

While my parents' relationship deteriorated and their fighting increased, I found more and more that Adi was the sunshine in my life. In the chaos of the hardship of living, he brought clarity along with the hope that life could get better, that my future might include a normal, happy existence.

In February, a time of year in Romania when sunshine is most needed, I was in my junior year and my mother agreed to let me go along with her and Nelu's girlfriend to visit Nelu at military school, which meant I'd get to see Adi as well. I was ecstatic. Talk of Adi led my mother to a furrowed brow and she'd bring the corners of her mouth down into a frown. She made no attempt to hide the fact that she wasn't too fond of Adi and had categorically rejected any of my requests to visit him.

There were a number of reasons for my mother's open disdain of Adi. Chief among them was that there was another young man in our town who had been courting me. It began when I was fifteen and he was eighteen, and though I sensed he was a good person and never doubted his affection for me, I felt smothered by him. His attention somehow highlighted how poor we were, living in an unfinished house with a backyard that turned to mud every time it rained. With him I felt ever conscious of my lack of nice clothes and our poverty in general. My mother thought the match was a good one, but I never felt the same draw to him (or as comfortable with him) as I did with Adi.

My mom also bristled at the fact that Adi never addressed her directly. He had a way of working around a conversation so that he was always in front of her when speaking to her, eliminating the need to call her by name or by something more informal. Though I would address Adi's mother as "Mom," he would never adopt the same practice with my mother, a detail that never sat well with her.

Despite all of her misgivings, she'd agreed to let me visit Adi and I couldn't have been happier. I planned the trip with a rich soul, but with poor clothing. I made a few attempts to improve my ragged wardrobe, including borrowing a warm coat from my cousin. My mother bought me a new pair of red and black boots. They were cheap, but didn't have any holes in them, so they were better than what I'd had before. I felt as if rich, dressed up like that in my new and borrowed clothes, but the cold was still brutal to me. My toes were numb with cold and my underclothes were insufficient to keep out the biting chill. But I was headed to Adi, my sunshine and my warmth.

The train trip was uneventful. The train slowly puffed along the tracks as I watched the small towns grow bigger. Branches of trees bent heavily with freezing snow as if something out of a fairytale. I wondered where the birds were hiding and how much longer until the spring would come, which was my favorite season. The world coming to life after a long cold winter brought joy to my soul.

As the train pulled into Alba Iulia, our station, my mom told us to get ready. We grabbed our bags and headed towards the door. As it opened, the chilled air hit my face and slowly seeped into my body again. It was a long walk up the hill to the military high school and we were all relieved when we finally made it there. It was Sunday, when the cadets could receive visitors. We were told to go to the waiting room where we'd find Adi and Nelu. A broad smile took over Adi's face when his playful eyes met mine. Our hands touched and we kissed, right there in front of my mother. We were too excited to see each other and unable to stifle our happiness. We stayed there talking and enjoying each other's company. Nelu and his girlfriend, an easygoing girl with dark hair, brown eyes, and a friendly demeanor, were equally enthralled with one another and had trouble keeping their hands off each other throughout the trip. Nelu's girlfriend was a friend of mine and I was happy for them both.

My mom gave Nelu a care package and after a while, all too soon, it was already time to head out. We'd eat at a restaurant before having to head back to the train station. Despite the cold, we took the walk back slow and at one point headed through a park. Adi and I held hands and walked slower than the others, lingering at the back of the group. I noticed a young woman walking towards us along the path. She looked well dressed in a long warm coat and tall black boots, none of which had holes in them. She floated gracefully and long hair cascaded down over her shoulders. As she got closer, I saw her face and took note of how beautiful she was. Adi saw her too and casually mentioned after she'd passed by that the two of them had dated, but only for three dates. What was it, I wondered, that made me special? Why would he choose me over someone like that, a rich and beautiful girl? How easily I underestimated myself and my worth.

We stopped in at a pub to warm ourselves and enjoy hot food on that cold winter's day. Despite all of my wishes to freeze time, like the frozen branches of the trees, it came time for us to head back to the train station. Adi and Nelu would accompany us there and say goodbye before they'd begin the trek back to the military school.

Once again, Adi and I fell to the back of the group, unintentionally letting the others walk farther and farther ahead. The more we walked, the farther away Nelu, his girlfriend, and my mother got from us. It began to snow and darkness fell. The snow falling quietly in the night created a halo around the lights. It was peaceful and majestic the way the flakes were dancing around the light and falling to the ground, enveloping both of us. We stopped at every light pole, looking up and admiring the snow falling gracefully. More flakes were dancing harmoniously, embracing each other. We hadn't noticed the splendor and peacefulness before, but it felt as if it existed for us. We could have stayed there forever, not feeling the cold as our souls were on fire. Though still dressed in that cheap pair of boots and the borrowed coat, I no longer felt poverty. I felt only pure love and care. Adi made me feel important, smart and worth knowing. I couldn't remember feeling like that ever before. My worries dispelled along with the fluffy snowflakes and a sheltered and intimate feeling took over.

The time flew without our knowledge and we couldn't have cared less. We were happy in a timeless space, in our space where no one could judge us and no one else could enter. It was the first time I didn't care about the world around me or about what it might be saying about me. Adi made me feel true to myself and showed me a better version of myself. He cared. Truly and deeply cared. He was sunshine, dawning on my life like the first day of the world.

When we realized what time it was and how late it was, we also realized that the train had likely already left the station. I was sure my mom and brother were worried about us not making it on time. I was wondering how I would get home and when the next train would come. I figured I'd have to sleep in the cold train station on an uncomfortable chair. Adi would have to make the walk back to school. We picked up our pace, throwing the worries and thoughts in a corner of our minds for a little longer. The evening was too wonderful to be upset about the real world and the reality of being stuck in a far away town without money and a plan of how to get home. I was falling in love.

When we entered the crowded train station we found the others.

"Where have you been?" my mom demanded. "Luckily, the

train was late because of the snow and it's pulling into the station now."

I couldn't help but think that fate was stepping in, delaying the train for us by bringing in the snowfall. The same weather that had enveloped Adi and me along our walk had changed the train's timetable in our favor. Relief embraced me like a warm fire and cozy blanket. I caught the train by chance and I was going home that night. I reluctantly said goodbye to Adi and my brother and boarded the train. As the train left the station, I opened the window to look back at the two silhouettes getting smaller by the second. My heart shrank into sadness. My smile disappeared as the reality of going back home and not seeing Adi for a while sank in. I would have to wait a full week to get a letter from him. I closed the window and sat down. Only then I realized how cold I was, how my fingers and toes were frozen as they adapted to the warmth of the cabin, trying to catch up with the warmth of my soul.

* * *

Spring passed slowly as I awaited the arrival of summer. After much convincing, my mother finally agreed to let me visit Adi's house, of course with the accompaniment of Nelu as a chaperone. We were to stay there for a week. As I anticipated the visit, I trembled at the thought of spending a full week with Adi...my Adi. We were deeply in love by that point, writing letters to each other every week, longing to spend more time together. I was seventeen years old and beginning my senior year, while Adi was preparing to begin his education in the Air Force College. It was his passion for flying that initially took him to military school. He was told that it would be the best path to get into the Air Force College. Even though he didn't like the idea of the military, he made the effort to fulfill his lifelong dream of flight. I was there for him along the admissions process and was overjoyed when he was accepted. His confidence during that time told me that he'd never expected any other outcome.

He was scheduled to start at the Air Force College on August 23, which was significant as it was Romania's Liberation Day, the day we celebrated liberation from fascist occupation, which was replaced by Soviet occupation. A day to commemorate going from one occupation to another.

Nelu and I took the train and I was overjoyed when I spotted Adi waiting for us at the station. We walked a few miles until we reached his parents' house up a curvy road on a hill.

On the way there was a beautiful church with a lovely veranda. Adi told us that his father had helped build it. During Communist times it was forbidden to build churches, as Communism didn't permit religion, but the government occasionally did grant permission for a crew to repair an old church. Adi's father told his crew that they'd received the government's permission. The crew, working fast so that their change of plans wouldn't be noticed, built a new church around the old one, instead of repairing the original church as they'd been commissioned. They finished the new church, then knocked down the old one inside. The townspeople got the new house of worship they'd wanted, which was a pushback against a government that repressed religion. A further twist in the tale came to light when the crew learned that Adi's father had never actually secured the permission as he'd purported. As a result, he was fired from his job as mayor as a disciplinary action.

We continued on and when we were almost at the top of the hill, the valley and the forest beyond it made their majestic appearance. Soaking in the tranquility and peacefulness of the view, with Adi by my side, I felt I could have stayed there forever.

At Adi's parents' house we opened an iron gate and found ourselves in the front yard, to the right of the main house. A few stairs led up to two rooms, a living room and hallway. Adi's mom graciously gave my brother and me the best room to sleep in.

A bit farther into the yard on the right side sat a small building that was later used for the kitchen and bathroom, though there was no toilet. Instead there was an outhouse not far from the kitchen. The back of the property was flanked by a long garden running down the hill, all the way to a small brook at the bottom. Vegetables, plum, and apple trees filled the garden, along with a line of raspberry bushes—Adi was fond of raspberry ice cream, which he would make himself.

Any apprehensions I'd had about meeting Adi's parents dissipated upon our arrival. His mother, Maria, was a petite woman, shorter than me, with her hair tied back and a scarf covering her head. Her blue eyes never looked at me with judgement, only with shock that Adi had actually found a girl that could steal his heart. Adi's father, Ion, was a small man who wore a perpetual smile and always had a joke at the ready. He trusted his son to make his own decisions. I felt nothing short of welcome in their home.

We spent a week together at his parents' house. Every day we went to the forest to run up and down the hills, where a river ran along the bottom. We would get our feet wet and Adi would splash me with the creek, or we'd venture deep into the forest to pick blackberries. Then we would kiss and hold hands, enjoying the rare time alone we had together.

Sometimes we'd come home hungry and eat lunch, but most of the time we were outdoors playing, biking or swimming. One day Nelu, Adi and I biked all the way up to Pădurea Neagră in the mountains. After biking 20 miles, the last few of which were uphill, we reached a mineral spring. We filled our little bottles of water and rested a bit before starting down the hill. Adi was a cyclist and he told my brother and me to be careful biking down the winding road. It was an abrupt trail with no rail for protection; one small mistake and you might end up at the bottom. I knew how to bike, but I wasn't an expert. Once I saw Adi hit the road, though, I just went down after him. I focused on the road and tried my best to not make mistakes. I felt the wind racing past my ears and chills run through my body. The adrenaline rushed through me. I tried to brake a bit here and there, but I was more worried about increasing the distance between Adi and me than I was about how fast I was moving. It didn't occur to me once that I was in danger or how good of a cyclist you had to be to get down that mountain at the speed I was racing. I reached the bottom, in one piece, right behind Adi. He thought he'd have time for a good rest before I arrived, but there I was right behind him. He was shocked to see me stopping next to him. He hugged me and I wasn't sure if it was because he thought I was brave or daring, or just because he was happy to see me alive. We waited quite a while until my brother made it down and then we all biked back home, exhausted, exhilarated, and content.

For the sake of propriety I shared a room with Nelu, but every night Adi would come visit to hug me and kiss me goodnight. As the week wore on, our goodbyes became longer and longer, keeping our hands off of each other grew more difficult. One night, while Nelu was sound asleep, we found it impossible to say goodbye. On impulse I ran my hand down to Adi's pants. He gasped and we froze for a moment in the dark. This was uncharted territory for us.

Worried that we would wake my brother, we snuck out of the room together, then out of the house and into the ink of the warm summer night. Our hands clasped tightly together, I felt the electricity between us, along with the uncertainty of the path ahead. My heart beat fast and strong in my chest, and I'm sure Adi's did the same.

He led me to the summer kitchen, a large room with a wood stove for cooking and keeping warm. Like most kitchens, it had a bed, used as an extra if one was needed near a heat source. I couldn't see anything in the darkness, but Adi knew the way and led me to the bed where we sank down into each other's arms. Our hands moved feverishly and I found myself unzipping Adi's pants. We had mixed feelings of wanting everything to stay as it was: perfect. At the same time, passion is undeniable. I wanted him. I wanted to let myself go with Adi. We both lost our virginity that night.

* * *

In the fall of 1984, I was in my senior year of high school while Adi was a freshman cadet at the Air Force College. I was back home in Salonta, while he was far away near a small village called Boboc. That fall our high school received permission to take a few students to Bucharest for a tour of TIBCO, a trade fair of consumer goods that drew exhibitors from many surrounding countries. To visit the capital city was exciting in itself; adding in an enormous trade show only heightened the anticipation of the students selected to go. While I looked forward to the trip, I also thought of how nice it would have been if Adi and I had been able to go together. Little did I know that miles away, my love was having the same thought.

My teacher, colleagues and I took the overnight train to Bucharest and then a subway to the TIBCO building the following day. A long road led to the main building, a round and imposing structure, the architecture of which was nothing like anything I'd ever seen before. It looked like a giant saucer from outer space, come to rest at the end of the long road before it might lift off and continue its journey to another galaxy. As my wide eyes moved from the impressive building to the path in front of me, I saw a group of students in blue military uniforms. Maybe they were aviators. My heart jumped at the tiny, ticklish thought…could they be Air Force College cadets? Or perhaps they were marines or from the Aviation Academy, either of which were also possibilities. But still, what if there was a chance that these were cadets from

Boboc? Could Adi be among their ranks?

It was an unthinkable idea and coincidence, but my hopes were high. I broke from our group, dragging my best friend along with me and ignoring her questions of where we were going. "Just come on," I pleaded.

We reached the group of blue-uniformed men and I looked around for someone who I might ask for information. I spotted a gray-haired man in his forties with friendly blue eyes and dared to ask him.

"Excuse me," I asked. "Can you tell me where your group is from?"

"We are from the Air Force College in Boboc," he answered, as my heart dared to take a further leap.

"Are the first-year cadets here, too?" I asked.

"Yes," he answered, "a few of them are here, too."

By the time his last words were spoken, my heart was jumping out of my chest. I pulled my friend, who now understood my sense of urgency, with me along the long road to the building. There was no sign of him anywhere. I entered the grandiose building with its rooms filled with endless wonders, but I saw none of it. My eyes searched only for my loved one.

There he was. With his best friend, exiting one of the exposition rooms and looking around for where they were headed next. I walked up to him and jumped in his arms. We were both speechless. What were the odds of us both going to Bucharest on the same day, at the same time, to the same place?

We spent the day holding hands while we browsed the exhibition. There was furniture and clothing, the quality of which I'd never seen before. "Do we really produce this?" I wondered aloud. "It's made in Romania?" There was new technology, the likes of which I didn't know existed. I was sure that everything must have been made in other countries. I couldn't imagine these wonders had been made in Romania. And they had, but only for export. The president wanted to pay the national debt. He did so, but the more he paid, the poorer we Romanians got.

The exhibition seemed impossible, as our stores were almost empty. The goods available to the average Romanian weren't anywhere near the quality of the goods before me. In addition, the government placed strict rations on the basic necessities of a kitchen, like oil, sugar, and meat. The exhibition shocked me, while Adi simply smiled at my surprise. Adi's father was the mayor of his rich oil village for sixteen years. His family had everything they needed and Adi wasn't deprived of anything growing up. Their family included four brothers and one sister, but they had a nice house full of everything they wanted or needed. Adi made trips across the country, and at fifteen was allowed to go with a few friends and one teacher, biking with just a small tent in his backpack. He wasn't spoiled because of his opportunities, but because of his upbringing, it was in his nature to reach for what his heart wanted, without second-guessing himself. He had the confidence of a king in his castle. Nothing seemed impossible to him, and so visiting the exposition didn't impress him in the same way it impressed me. He would giggle at my innocence in discovering new worlds of possibilities. He was curious too, and a lot of things were new to him as well, but the big difference was in our expectations. He expected it would be like that. I had no idea what to expect. Not from the exposition, nor from life itself.

5

DON'T JUDGE A BOOK BY ITS COVER

The March day was cold and rainy, the remains of winter still clinging in the air, resisting the oncoming spring. As soon as I saw Adi unexpectedly show up in the backyard with his radiant smile, I felt a warmth wash over my soul despite the chill of the weather. I was ecstatic at his presence and curious about the light in his eyes, as if he was always up to something that I hadn't quite yet figured out. That was Adi, never obvious but always acting with purpose, following an agenda at which you could never guess.

We spent the weekend strolling through town together and slowly, on long walks and in conversations, the reason for his surprise visit began to reveal itself. He described the process for admission into Air Force College, but he spoke with surprising detail about the medical examinations, the physical challenges, and the scope of knowledge needed in physics, math, and geography. He detailed the admission process as if weaving a fairytale. At first I thought this was simply because flying had been his dream since boyhood, but then realized there was another part of the conversation yet to come. Adi told me that for the first time in history, the Romanian Air Force would allow a class for women pilots, limited to only twenty seats. Elena Ceaușescu, Communist politician and wife of Nicolae Ceaușescu, had taken note of the lack of women in the Air Force and advocated for the policy to change. A lack of access to widespread media kept this historic decision largely under wraps. The only people who knew of it were those already close to the politics of military policy.

Until that moment, I had never considered becoming a pilot or shared Adi's desire to fly. But when Adi and I fell in love, his dreams became mine and vice versa. Our lives were inextricably intertwined and our desires merged into a shared life.

Adi never implicitly asked me to apply to the Air Force College. He never urged me to pursue this new possibility in life. He simply laid the facts before me, planting the seeds of thoughts in my mind. At the end of the weekend, before he left to return to college, he looked into my eyes and said, "If you were to apply and go through the process, I am sure you would get in, Rodica. You are very smart and capable." That was my Adi. He never pushed, but he gave me pieces of the puzzle and then left me to assemble them. He was like a teacher who would never admit that he was filling that role for me. At that moment he initiated a wish inside my soul, but left me to follow through with it on my own. He was amazing at recognizing my potential and bringing it to the surface, but allowing me to bring it to life through my own power.

In hindsight I can see how he filled a void in my life. Adi gently offered guidance that I'd never received from my parents. Nelu and I had depended on each other growing up, had taught one another as best we could in our parents' absence, but he'd left home at fourteen. With Adi I found the partner I'd been missing.

Up until that point, I'd planned on taking the entrance exams for the Economics Academy in Bucharest. Could I really change course so late in the game? I wasn't strong in physics and hadn't been studying geography in depth because it wasn't applicable to my chosen field. With Adi back at college, I had only myself with whom to mull over this decision. I said nothing to my parents, sure that they would persuade me out of it, and consulted only my own conscience. Air Force College certainly sounded more exciting than the Economics Academy. It would also converge Adi's life path with my own. Above all, the chance to be a member of the first female Air Force class in the history of the Romanian military was a once-in-a-lifetime opportunity. How could I give up without even trying? I had to go for it. I made up my mind to apply. If I didn't make the cut, I could always go back to my original plan the following year.

The next day I skipped school and without telling anyone took the train to the military unit in the next town, so that I could register for the admission process. When I approached the unit, there was a soldier posted at the gate. I told him why I was there, and he informed me that the admission process was closed; it was too late to apply. The idea of a dream dashed so early felt like a blow to my chest. My eyes welled with tears. "Please let me talk to the colonel in charge," I begged. "Please."

Recognizing my desperation, he said, "Well, I don't think there's anything he can do for you, but okay, you can go talk to him."

He let me pass and led me to the colonel's office, where a man in his fifties sat behind a heavy wooden desk. "Yes?" he asked. "What is it you need?"

"I'd like to apply for military college," I said, choking back the tears.

"Applications are closed," he responded. "Sorry, but we can't process any more, it's too late."

I steeled myself with resolve and decided I wouldn't take no for an answer. I would leave his office only when I was allowed to apply. Repeating my plea over and over, he kept responding that I was simply too late. "Please," I said. "You can just squeeze me in."

He sighed and focused on me, measuring my grit. "Which military college?" he asked.

"Air Force."

"Oh! You don't want to apply to just any military college, you want the Air Force?"

"Yes."

He sized me up again and then relented with another sigh. "Fine," he said. "What the hell, one more application. There were so many, one more won't matter anyway."

I felt a weight rise from my shoulders and lightness flood through my chest. The colonel gave me the paperwork to take to the hospital where I'd face a barrage of medical exams. If I passed the medical portion of the process, I was to return to him for the next phase of admissions, during which he'd send me to the Institute of Aeronautical Medicine in Bucharest. He wished me luck.

I left the colonel's office with a mixture of elation and fear at what may lay ahead. The soldier at the gate asked me what had happened, and shook his head in disbelief when I told him that I'd been permitted to apply.

When I returned home, I still kept my new plan to myself. I wasn't ready to tell my parents about my change of heart or that I'd gone to a military unit that day instead of to school as usual. Only when I returned from Oradea, having passed the medical exams, did I dare to reveal my plans. My mother didn't say much. My father wanted me to succeed no matter what path I took. I was determined not to disappoint him. Only later would I learn that despite my father's words of encouragement to me, he told Adi in private that if I failed, it would prove that I wasn't worthy of Adi.

* * *

Nervous excitement filled my heart during the train ride to Bucharest. I traveled by myself, just a little girl from a small town headed to the big city and determined to succeed. Nelu and Adi met me at the train station, as we had a few hours together before I'd report to my destination, a large building dedicated entirely to hopeful future pilots undergoing medical examinations. Standing outside the building, I confessed my waning confidence. My determination to succeed was beginning to erode.

"Look at the other girls going into the building," I said, trying to hold back tears. "They all look so confident and prepared. I bet most of them already know about aviation or have relatives in the

Air Force. I don't stand a chance."

Both Adi and Nelu tried to comfort me and bring a smile to my face, but in the end it was up to me. They had to leave me to move forward on my own. As they left that day, I felt my heart in pieces, doubting my ability to put it back together and muster the strength to go on. With one foot in front of the other, I set my shoulders back, wiped away my fears, and took that first step.

The top floor of the building served as our dormitory. I was surrounded by strong, determined girls from all over Romania. Many of them had nice new clothes while I'd been scrambling to gather the money for the train ticket. My new surroundings were overwhelming, not least of all when it came time to shower. I had never been naked in front of other people. The large communal shower provided little hiding space for me, and I always bathed as quickly as possible so that I could return to the comfort of clothing.

Upon arrival, each of the candidates was issued a booklet that detailed the tests we had to pass...or fail. After an examination, we would receive a stamp in our booklet saying that we had passed. At the end of every day, we'd gather in the dormitory and compare our booklets, finding out who had passed their exams and who would be sent home. And so every evening our numbers would dwindle as girls were sent home, often leaving in tears as they learned that their dreams of being in the Romanian Air Force were dashed.

As the evenings passed and I continually kept my spot in the group, my confidence grew back.

For five days we were physically and mentally tested. The written psychology exam took a full day and would be graded only after we'd all returned home. Then we were given the practical psychology test. The psychiatrist was a woman in her forties who radiated peace and calm. During the test I admired her beauty and marvelled at how comfortable I felt around this woman who, only moments before, had been a complete stranger to me.

She sat me down in front of a very small screen and an accompanying joystick. This was to test agility, concentration, and dexterity, as well as a cadet's ability to think and react quickly. I was to track a red dot by moving the controls, but as soon as I'd figure out how the joystick worked, she would change the format of the controls. So I'd track the red dot after learning that the controls worked one way, only to have the rules switched on me. This was long before the current world of technology and cell phones and video games, so I'd never experienced anything like the test and wasn't really sure how I was doing. That's when the kind woman spoke.

"Keep going," she whispered. "You already passed the test long ago, but if you keep going like this you might break the record." There was a smile in her eyes and I knew that she was rooting for me. I did end up breaking the record and for the rest of my time there, though the woman would pretend not to recognize me in the hallways, I'd catch a slight smile from her and again note that her eyes looked upon me with a kindness she didn't offer to the other cadets. In the years that followed, when I'd have to return for the annual medical exams, she always acknowledged me with that same kindness, an affirmation that she was happy I'd succeeded.

My nerves increased when it came time to enter the barometric chamber. The worst part was that there was no way to prepare, we simply had to hope that our bodies could handle a lack of oxygen and decrease in pressure. My heart pounded as I was strapped into my chair and staff placed monitors on me to track my pulse and heart rate.

We'd heard that the key was to keep talking in order to stay awake. There were eight of us in the barometric chamber during the test and we nervously all spoke at the same time, sharing the hope that we could endure it without passing out. We climbed incredibly fast and as the air grew thinner we began gasping just to try to keep taking in oxygen. We had no idea when it would end, when the pressure would normalize and we'd be able to breathe again. The room turned quiet and I focused on staying conscious, when suddenly we heard a voice over the speaker say, "Okay, get ready, we're going to bring you down now." Sweeter words had never been spoken. Coming down was still an ordeal—I had to swallow more often and felt the continuing vertigo—but the knowledge that it was almost over felt like pure joy. Relief washed over me as the pressure and oxygen levels returned to normal.

As I exited the chamber, sweaty, dizzy, and drained, it hit me: I had passed. But my ordeal was not over yet. I still had another challenging test before me, which was the gyro chair. I stood in line with the other girls who still remained in the program, waiting for my turn. I watched the other candidates take their turns, one by one sitting in what looked like a dentist's chair, but which could be rotated in either direction at different speeds. We had to close our eyes while the chair would be rotated left, stopped, and then rotated right and stopped again before the process would start again from the beginning. Every time the chair stopped we were told to hold our arms in front of us with our eyes still closed while we endured the test. In front of me in line, I watched as three girls in a row completed the test, but then immediately vomited into a bucket nearby, kept for just such purpose. Each time a girl got sick, that was another failure and another dream dashed. My nerves skyrocketed when it came to be my turn, but my stomach held strong and I managed to hold my hands up with small variances of movement. And once again, I passed.

As I walked up the stairs to the dormitory that evening, the reality of my situation began to sink in. It was becoming a reality. I understood then while Adi's Air Force ambitions were to fulfill a lifelong dream to fly, I was in a different position. I was standing on the brink of history, gaining wings that would lead me to be one of the first twenty women to become pilots in the Romanian Air Force. Being part of something so unique felt like a privilege.

Being able to do so with Adi by my side made my love for him grow into a shared love of flying.

I left Bucharest thinking that I'd done well, but only time would tell for sure. I had to wait to find out if I'd passed the written psychological exam. Mail was scarce in those days and we didn't have any sort of mailbox. An occasional letter from a distant relative or a letter from Adi was all we would receive, with such mail simply being thrown through the gate and onto the small path beside our house. When the little postcard arrived in the mail letting me know that I'd passed all of the medical tests, I was elated. Now I had athletic testing, physics, math, and geography to pass if I wanted to stay in the running. By that time the original applying cadets had been whittled from over a thousand down to around four hundred. Could I really end up with one of those twenty coveted spots?

While I wanted to be in the same college as Adi and be close to him, while also doing something women hadn't done before, I didn't yet dare to dream that it might become a reality. I knew that my chances were slim and many challenges still lay before me.

At that moment, the challenge at hand was physics. It wasn't my strongest skill, nor was it my favorite, but I needed to act fast and buckle down if I was to have a chance at completing the next leg of my journey. I decided to ask for help. I went to my physics teacher, explained my dilemma, and he presented me with his personal notebooks from all four years of high school physics classes, complete with exercises and solutions. His notes, written in meticulous handwriting, provided me with everything I needed. Basically I had two months to learn four years of physics, refresh my math knowledge, and gain a complete understanding of geography. Rather than stress about the task before me, I got to work.

The next portion of tests took place in Buzau, and this time my father accompanied me for the journey there. He was beginning to take my dream seriously, realized what it meant to me, and wanted to make sure I arrived safely. He also made contact with an acquaintance from Air Force College, Lieutenant Colonel Grigore Chioreanu who, along with his wife Vali, took me in. I will forever be grateful that he took pity on me and offered advice, a hot meal and a bed to sleep in.

Testing began with basic pass/fail athletics tests, along with a test per day in either math, physics, or geography. We began with running, and what may seem like such a simple act had me more worried than anything else that was to come. Often when I ran I experienced a painful cramp in my side, and I worried that this would return and hinder my performance. *Breathe*, I told myself. *Just breathe.*

During the written tests I sat at a desk in a large room with the other candidates. My anxiety was always greatest waiting for the test to begin, wondering how I would perform, but once testing began, I always managed to focus and summon the knowledge I'd worked so hard to cultivate in the previous two months.

Adi would come to see me whenever he could (so much so that some of his colleagues initially thought we were brother and sister) and the sight of him filled me with a warmth and reassurance that kept me focused on the tasks at hand. When the results were posted, I didn't dare look. What if my dreams were coming to an end? It was Lieutenant Colonel Grigore Chioreanu who went to look and brought home the news. I'd made it. Along with nineteen other women, I would be part of the first graduating class of female Air Force pilots. While I felt relief at the end of the difficult process and revelled in the feelings of having successfully been selected as one of the final twenty, I also felt worry and uncertainty about the road ahead. One thing was for certain; I was about to make history.

Later I learned from my best girlfriend at high school that while I'd been undergoing tests in Bucharest, including the dreaded barometric chamber and the gyro chair, a military recruiter had visited my high school back home, hoping to recruit some young cadets. While no one in my class was interested, one of my classmates volunteered the information that I had applied to military school. The recruiter asked which one, and when my fellow students told him it was Air Force college, the recruiter began to laugh. And then the students joined in as well. To them it was a joke, this mocking of my dreams. Little did they know the extent of my determination. Only two months after I imagined their laughter fading into the hallways of the high school, I was accepted into the Romanian Air Force College.

6

WHERE THERE'S A WILL, THERE'S A WAY

The Romanian Air Force College, Aurel Vlaicu, was located fifteen kilometers from Buzau, close to Boboc village. The cadets would take the local train from Buzau to the Boboc station, where we'd disembark to drag ourselves and luggage another two kilometers to the aviation unit. We'd spend four years at Aurel Vlaicu, graduating as lieutenants with degrees in electrical engineering.

My college years were filled with studying, flying, and of course my relationship with Adi. In the first year, cadets flew the IAR-823, a small, four-seater plane used for screening and developing basic aviation skills.

In the beginning, we assumed that our unit of female aviators would follow the same path as that of the male cadets, but we were mistaken. A general from Bucharest arrived in our classroom one day, informing us of a change in plan. "Girls," he said, "we've decided to have you fly helicopters so you won't have to worry about spilling your coffee." I felt the heat of quiet outrage fill the room. We were being tasked with the Alouette, the IAR-316B helicopter, while our male counterparts would be moving on to the L-29 Delfin jet. We felt both frustrated and discriminated against. We'd been preparing to fly jets. We were fit and ready to fly jets. Though some of my classmates voiced their outrage, the general explained that as the first female class of pilots, the decision had been made to be careful with our assignments, and the decision was also final.

While I was frustrated with this new path, I was not as troubled as many of my colleagues. I'd looked forward to flying jets, but still felt that even being there, in the Air Force College and in the same college as Adi, was ultimately a privilege. With that recognition, I also decided that I would embrace flying helicopters, though a little resentment lingered over the general's remark about sparing us the jets so that we wouldn't spill our coffee.

Despite the discriminatory flight path, our commanders did put forth effort to ensure our comfort. They brought in a female lieutenant as our platoon commander and restored a building from World War II to serve as our dwelling. We had six apartments, each with two common rooms, a kitchen, and a bathroom dedicated to our female class, while the men continued living in the main dormitories.

The college had two main buildings for studies, one for non-flying cadets and where the staff offices were located, and the building for the pilot cadets. Once again, the female class would find ourselves being treated differently than our male counterparts. Instead of training us in the building for pilot cadets, we were relegated to the building of staff offices and non-flying cadets. The reasoning we were given is that the pilots were a corrupt and messy lot. Our group, by comparison, was disciplined and studious. To keep us from being corrupted by the unruly pilots, we'd be kept separate in the main building, where we "belonged."

Where I truly belonged, in addition to Air Force College, was with Adi, and our lives became more and more intertwined during the college years. Adi would visit me during every break, constantly running back and forth between the two buildings to see me. So much so that, at one point, one of the teachers exited our classroom as the class finished, saw Adi waiting patiently for me in the hallway, and said, "Ponici, leave Corha alone. You're here all the time."

Of course, what felt like "all the time" to others felt like never enough time to Adi and me. Our breaks were brief and our studies ate up so much of our available time. To be fair, it was more me studying than Adi. While I had favorite subjects, navigation in particular, all of the subjects came naturally to Adi, so much so that he didn't need to devote extra time to his studies. He had a talent not only for understanding the material, but also for explaining it. So many times he would sit with me and explain aerodynamics or the mechanics of a plane engine or meteorology. The studies based on physics were never my forte; Adi devoured it all.

In the early days of college, Adi would come visit me at my apartment, which I shared with three roommates. The four of us shared two bedrooms. Over time Adi began staying the night, and before long we were inseparable. None of my roommates balked at Adi's constant presence. His smile was infectious and it didn't take long for them to consider him an adopted fifth roommate.

We were close to the same clothing size, and on more than one occasion Adi rushed out in the morning, not realizing he'd grabbed one of my shirts by mistake. His colleagues joked that he'd downgraded himself in rank the day he accidentally grabbed one of my corporal rank shirts, thinking it was his own. Of course, Adi was not the only cadet with a girlfriend at college, but it was well known that the two of us were together nearly all the time.

Impromptu inspections were common, with one colonel in particular determined to catch one of the guys in the girls' dorm. One night Adi had to quickly hide in the attic. When the colonel went up to the attic, I figured we were done for, but Adi stayed hidden and eventually the colonel left. Despite the close call, he never stopped coming to see me.

One night during the summer, a duty officer caught us while we were having a small party in our common room. The guys took off running. The girls were questioned about which guys had been there, but our lips were sealed. We refused to give names. As punishment, College Commander General Mereu instructed that the following day, instead of flying, we would march, hauling equipment along the way. Before marching, we were to get up early in the morning and begin sweeping the paths in front of the main building.

While we didn't look forward to the general's punishment of marching instead of flying on that beautiful day, we dreaded even more having to tell our flight instructors of the change in plan and why we'd landed ourselves in trouble. None of us wanted our instructors looking down on us or thinking less of us. When they got off of their bus and saw us sweeping, brooms in hand, they asked us what was going on. We told them the truth and to our relief, they weren't mad at all. They readied themselves and marched with us. Though marching twenty kilometers with gear on a hot summer day was intended as punishment, we sang songs together, managed to have a great time, and returned not only in one piece, but also in high spirits.

That same summer, after logging in less than ten hours of flight time, I was told I was ready for my first solo flight. Just me and the airplane. I was nervous but excited, and hardly slept the night before in anticipation of the flight. I kept repeating the steps and emergency procedures over and over to myself. Arriving at the airfield the next day, my first thought was, *What a bright, amazing day.* Everything seemed shinier than usual. I went through flight preparations and inspection, then climbed into the plane with mixed emotions. I was determined to do well and reminded myself that I had the invaluable ability to remain calm under pressure.

Taking off was easy. I completed my flight and prepared for landing. I wasn't afraid, but focused and determined to land safely. When I touched the wheels down and taxied back, I saw Adi there waiting to give me a congratulatory hug. My female colleagues then took me for the ritual of baptism by thorns. It was customary after completing a solo flight. The pilot's colleagues would gather as many thorny plants as they could and place them in a big pile, then grab the pilot by the arms and legs and drag them in all directions with their backs over the thorns. The girls did this with our flight suits on, so we felt it but it didn't really hurt. It was more of a playful ritual. The guys, on the other hand, made the pilot remove his shirt and the lucky soloist would often end up in the nurse's office afterward to get thorns removed from his back.

Boboc's winters were harsh, an onslaught of snow and freezing temperatures. As we battled the cold, I couldn't help but feel grateful for the warmth in my heart. The men's dorm didn't have much heat. We had electric heaters in the women's apartments, but soon learned that the World War II-era circuits weren't capable of keeping up with the demand for extra electricity. Luckily, Adi was always there to fix the circuits when they went down. Though he could have waited for someone else to tackle the job, he always volunteered, insisting that if he fixed the circuits, he could be sure that I'd be warm. "I can't wait for others to fix the problem," he explained, "because if they don't, you'll be cold." Adi always took my comfort to heart and put it before his own needs.

In addition to flying, we also had to study military subjects. After all, we were to graduate as officers. Lieutenant Colonel Chioreanu oversaw the shooting training. I enjoyed target practice, as I knew I was good at it, dating all the way back to that day in high school when I first held a rifle in Oradea.

Soldiers were on hand to assist Lieutenant Colonel Chioreanu and I learned that sometimes, when a cadet struggled to hit a target after a few tries, the soldiers would secretly hit a lever that would lower the target, leading the shooter to believe they'd finally hit their mark. Whenever it was my turn, I would fiercely hope that the soldiers wouldn't take down my target so that I could hit in on my own merit. Much later, after I graduated, I asked Lieutenant Colonel Chioreanu about this. "I always did my best," I said, "but I need to know if you ever told the soldiers to take my targets down or if they fell because I hit them."

The lieutenant colonel looked at me and with pride in his voice and explained, "Not only did I withhold the order to take down your targets, but I also told the soldiers your line number and that if they dared to take down your targets, they would be punished. I wanted you to do well on your own merits. And you did amazing."

His words, and above all his respect, meant the world to me.

* * *

From fall to late spring we were busy studying, while the rest of the time was spent flying. As first-year cadets, our food was calculated at 4,500 calories per day, but we never seemed to have enough. In the second year, since we were flying helicopters which were considered in the "jet" category, our caloric intake was upped to 5,500 calories per day. Still, we were no strangers to the feeling of hunger.

The food provided didn't include much variation, it was simply sustenance on which to survive. One evening during the first year, Adi came to visit me at the dining hall. The cooks were serving mutton, and the smell of the meat from the sheep permeated the cafeteria. It was near nauseating, but we were all hungry and determined to get whatever food into our bodies that we could. When Adi arrived and the smell hit him, he looked at me about to consume the putrid meal, then asked me to go with him. After adeptly bribing the cook for a few potatoes and eggs, we left the stench of the dining hall and went to my apartment. The eggs and potatoes we cooked and ate that evening were some of the tastiest foods I've ever had.

Our rations included a small square of chocolate every day. Instead of eating it, we'd save it up in a stash and then continue bribing the cooks, ten squares of chocolate at a time, for food that we could prepare in my apartment instead of suffering through whatever meal was being served that day. Though these instances didn't happen often, we felt spoiled when they did, along with a notable lift to our spirits.

Some cadets were still close to home and had the luxury of returning to their mothers' kitchens for meals. Often they'd bring extra food back to campus to share with the rest of us. A favorite indulgence was when we would go to Buzau and visit Lieutenant Colonel Chioreanu's house. His wife Vali was an amazing cook and generous in supplementing our less than desirable rations from the college. I always marveled at her ability to quickly whip up plates of delicious, fulfilling food from just a few ingredients. Vali was a petite lady in her late fifties, stocky with extra weight. "It's always good as you get older to have a few extra kilos," she advised us. "You never know when you might get sick and need those extra kilograms." She was a delightful person to be around, always cheerful and ready to help. While it wasn't common for cadets to visit the homes of their supervisors, the lieutenant colonel had promised my father he'd watch over me, a promise he was determined to keep.

When their granddaughter Ana-Maria would visit, the lieutenant colonel's wife would make her granddaughter try on skirts that she'd sewn, each with an elastic waistband. "You don't really have a waist yet," she'd tell Ana-Maria. "You are still growing. An elastic band will do for now." Ana-Maria would smile as she twirled to show off her new skirt.

Their home was a refuge for us, a place where we felt welcome and were always assured to be fed properly. We never wanted to overstay our welcome, though their door was always open to us. It was difficult to visit Buzau without stopping to admire both his flower garden and her cooking.

During my years at Air Force College I saw the beauty of being with Adi, the joy of caring for someone and being cared for in return, especially while we were so far from the comforts of home.

Though Adi's family had money by Romanian standards, his father left his mother to start a new life far away, leaving behind, among other things, financial strain. My own parents had no money to spare; it was hard on them having raised four kids on small salaries. My mother sent packages and money on occasion to Nelu at the Military Academy in Bucharest, but there was likely nothing remaining after she did so.

As such, Adi and I had little to no financial support from our parents, and the army provided little allowance, so we were often without money. Once, after a brief visit, Adi's father handed him 500 lei, and Adi's face sunk into sadness. The amount was equivalent to what you might pay a babysitter, and a fraction of what we truly needed.

"He knows how difficult this is on us, but this is all he gave us," Adi lamented. We were badly in need but rarely asked for help. Once I asked my father's sister Floarea for money. She was a woman of few words, a hard-worker without complaint. When we told her we needed 1,000 lei she looked deeply into our eyes and quietly left the room. When she returned she handed us the money, no questions asked. She simply said that she was glad she had the money in the house to be able to help. We never forgot her generosity.

Under Communism, we had six-day workweeks, with Sundays to ourselves. In the summer we would sometimes ask permission to leave the Air Force College. We'd venture to Sarata-Monteoru, a small vacation village on top of the hills close to Buzau, or we'd journey to Bucharest to visit Nelu. During our trips to Sarata-Monteoru, we'd overnight in a small wood cabin that fit only a twin bed and wasn't big enough to stand up straight in. We had little food with us, perhaps a piece of bacon and a slice of bread, but instead of focusing on our poverty, we dwelled in the happiness of being together and being away from the Air Force College. The river flowed, birds sang, and the sun warmed our bodies. It seemed as if it all existed just for us in those moments.

The day after one such journey, we headed to the Buzau train station. I would travel to Boboc and Adi to Focsani, another location for flight training. As we walked from the bus station to the train station, we passed a small ice cream parlor. The summer sun was intense and ice cream would have been quite welcome, but we only had ten lei, which we needed to bribe the train conductor. We rarely had money for train fare, so we'd try to avoid the conductor altogether and, when that wasn't possible, bribe him with whatever money we did have.

The ice cream was too much to resist. We bought two ice creams at 3 lei each, leaving 4 lei to bribe the train conductor, if needed. In my excitement over the ice cream, I promptly dropped mine onto the hot pavement, and could have cried right there. Adi shared his with me and then bought us another one, now leaving only one lei.

"Don't worry," Adi assured me. "I'll fool the train conductor. If he does see me, I'll just run."

It was common practice for the aviation cadets to bribe the conductors with just one lei on the trip from Buzau to Boboc. Once, when taking such a trip, we were in a good mood and decided we'd give the conductor five lei instead of two, one for each of us. The train conductor opened our compartment door, placing one foot inside and one out. He leaned on the doorframe and looked at us. Adi smiled and handed him the five lei, feeling good about our spontaneous generosity. The conductor took the money, then stared at us for what felt like an eternity. The moment reached a crescendo of tension when he opened the corridor window and threw the money out of the chugging train.

"I can't believe you officers would only give me five lei," he snarled.

We were shocked. We anticipated a more favorable reaction and were stunned that he mistook us for officers; we were merely cadets! The rank on our uniforms clearly designated us as cadets, but the conductor paid no attention to that. As he closed the door behind him, I wondered what else we might have done with that five lei that was now lost forever.

Another time we took what little money we had in our pockets and went to the post office to buy a pen. On returning to the dorms, we realized that the pen's ink was dry. There was no concept of returning items in those days, and once again we had to accept the fact that what little money we had was gone, with nothing in return. Without knowing it, we were building up a bank of painful memories of what it's like not to be able to afford the basic amenities of life.

* * *

The aerodynamics professor at the College was a first lieutenant, a calm and confident man whom many of my classmates thought to be good looking. I only had eyes for Adi, of course, and even when it came to airplane aerodynamics, I trusted Adi's word more than that of the professor. One day I even went so far as to challenge the professor on basic aerodynamic theory, which Adi had explained to me differently. The professor didn't like that one bit.

The professor and Adi's mutual dislike culminated when the first lieutenant invited me and another colleague to an aviation exhibition in Medias. Adi confronted him about his intentions and told the superior to leave me alone.

"Rodica is free to do what she wants," the professor replied.

"Yes," Adi conceded. "She can go if she wants to, but this isn't over between the two of us. I won't be a cadet forever, and when I graduate, I'm going to come and find you."

I'd learn about this conversation much later in life; at the time I had no idea why my name was suddenly withdrawn from the roster of exhibition attendees. Meanwhile, Adi had good reason to fear repercussions of his threat. Adi received low marks on his next two exams, despite the fact that he excelled in the aerodynamics course. It was clear that the professor wasn't going to disclose their confrontation, but was instead determined to fail him. As the final oral exam approached, Adi knew he had to receive high marks in order to pass the course. He also knew that the head of the college sometimes sat in on the oral examinations. No one wanted the added pressure of having the general present when delivering their final exam, except for Adi. He wanted a witness to his performance so that the first lieutenant would have no excuse to issue him a failing grade.

Normally we chose numbers out of a hat to determine the order in which we'd take our exams, but Adi's fellow cadets conspired with him so that he'd have his turn in front of the general. But when Adi prepared to deliver his exam, the general stood to leave.

In desperation, Adi pleaded, "General Commander, don't you want to hear my exam as well?"

The general stopped and turned around, reconsidering. "Of course I will," he said.

After Adi expertly delivered his exam, the general commented, "Very nicely done! You know your stuff," before taking his leave. That left little room for the first lieutenant to manipulate the grades and Adi received the well-deserved highest mark, a ten.

Sometimes Adi got in trouble of his own doing, and other times I was part of the problem. That first summer, while I was training at Boboc, Adi was training at Ianca on the L-29 Delfin. In a brief bout of homesickness, I was granted permission for a three-day leave to return home and visit my family. Without the ease of cell phones and internet, I was unable to reach Adi to tell him of my plans. When he arrived at Boboc that Saturday to visit me and learned that I'd left, he felt concerned. He jumped on the next train to follow me and make sure I was alright, but the journey to Salonta required taking three different trains over the course of an entire night, and Adi didn't have enough money to buy all of the tickets or even bribe three different conductors. On the first two trains, while the other travelers slept through the night, Adi spent the ride running from conductors and trying to stay hidden. On the third train, he knew he needed a new plan. He had to have a ticket for the passage from Timisoara to Salonta. The ticket cost 22.50 lei and Adi only had 20. In a desperate attempt to make up the difference, he went to a pay phone, put in 25 bani, and hoped that when he hung up, more money would fall down the return chute. And it did. Exactly that 2.50 lei that he needed. He quickly bought the ticket and jumped onto the train at the last minute, as it was pulling out of the station.

I was shocked to see Adi arrive at my home in the early morning hours and knew immediately, from the stress telegraphed by his expression, that I'd caused a panic.

"Are you okay, Rodica? What's wrong?" he asked.

"Nothing is wrong," I explained. "I just wanted to visit my parents and brothers."

Since he hadn't asked for permission to leave his training in Ianca, he had to leave that night to get back. From Oradea he caught an express train. The plan was to take it to Fetesti, where he'd transfer to a local train to complete the journey to Ianca. What he didn't realize was that the train was an international train with no plans of stopping at Fetesti. He watched as the train passed by Fetesti with no hint of slowing down. In a split decision he pulled the emergency alarm cord. The train slowed to a stop, Adi pushed open the heavy door, then hopped down off the train with the intent of walking back to Fetesti and continuing his journey from there. But as soon as he disembarked from the train, he heard soldiers shouting and dogs barking. The international trains were subject to heavy surveillance to prohibit defectors. What began as a quick trip to check up on his girlfriend turned into a chase scene right out of a Hollywood movie, Adi running with heart pounding, hoping not to be suddenly tackled from behind by a German shepherd.

Running in darkness is difficult enough as it is, even more so when you're focused on outrunning dogs. To make matters worse, Adi made out a patch of darkness in his path that differed from the surrounding terrain. Figuring it was a stream, he picked up speed and prepared to hurtle over the running water. As he leapt into the air, his body was suddenly confronted with the harsh reality of a hill, not a stream, which he'd launched himself into. He moaned in pain for a moment, scared to move so that he could put off learning the extent of the damage he'd caused to his body. His only consolation, in that moment, was the faded sound of barking dogs, followed by the train chugging back to life as it continued on its journey without him.

Adi's night was far from over. After realizing that he was still in one piece, he began walking toward a grouping of lights in the distance until, at 2:00 a.m., he reached the Fetesti train station. With no trains running at that time of night, he curled up as best he could to sleep on a cold wooden chair.

Before morning broke, he was able to board a local train that would deliver him back to the Ianca station where he could hopefully return to his dorm undetected. It was still dark when he entered the train compartment, and none of the passengers could see very well in the pre-dawn light, though Adi heard a number of them inquiring, "What's that horrible smell?"

When he disembarked at Ianca, and the sun began its ascent, he realized not only that he was covered in mud, but also that he had undoubtedly been the source of the unpleasant smell the other passengers had complained about. Beyond that, his clothes were also torn from the ordeal, making it look as if he was returning to the base after completing a tour of duty in a war zone. But he knew he was almost home free, if he could just jump through the dormitory window, get cleaned up and sneak into the morning assembly, where his fellow cadets were already in formation. As Adi maneuvered through the dorm window, however, he found himself nose to nose with his flight commander.

"Where have you been?" the commander asked. "Why are you late reporting for duty?"

Adi confessed that he'd traveled to Salonta to see me. The commander stood silently for a moment, measuring the situation, then turned and left without another word. Adi quickly cleaned up and then reported for duty at the assembly, relieved that his adventure would go unreported, and exhausted after his two sleepless nights on the road.

Such graciousness from commanders was not uncommon. The bond that's created through flight is something that can't be seen or articulated, but is undeniably present. It existed between the pilot cadets and flight instructors in a way not present in other parts of the military. While we cadets tried to behave, we also hoped in our hearts for leniency when we did get in trouble, and were also grateful for that leniency when and if we were lucky enough to experience it.

* * *

Though Romania's first class of female Air Force aviators began at twenty, only nineteen of us would graduate. In our second year, one of my colleagues was dismissed from Air Force College. She was treated unfairly in the situation, but in Communist times, under the rule of Elena and Nicolae Ceaușescu, many things happened which never should have. She was dismissed from the military, along with the dreams of flying that had coursed through her veins. Many years later, after the fall of Communism, she was permitted to attend civilian aviation college and turn her passion of flying into a reality.

My initial attempts to be an aviator stemmed from my desire to be with Adi, but over time flying grew on me. My skills were perfectly suited for it and I wanted to be there with all my heart, but I also admired those who were there driven purely by their passion for flight. In addition, the ability to take part in a pioneering moment in history is difficult to describe. Only years later would my colleagues compare stories and realize the full extent of the trials we experienced during those times. There was so much for us to overcome, especially when compared with our male counterparts.

The bond between the twenty of us cadets, even after our colleague was dismissed, was as strong as any I've known. Despite varied backgrounds and upbringings, we were united by our strength of character and will, and most of all unified by our unique dream of flying. It was in our bond that we each realized we were worthy of being there, and so too we were there for each other.

7

THERE'S A FIRST TIME FOR EVERYTHING

In the summer of 1986 I was nineteen years old, one of a few female cadets of the Air Force College of Romania, and about to experience one of the most remarkable and unforgettable moments of my life.

I'd been in college for almost a year. My colleagues and I were growing more excited by the day, as we'd finished our theoretical courses for the year and now would get more practical, hands-on instruction: we were going to learn how to fly.

We'd only had a few hours of flight instruction under our belts the day the parachutist instructor came to our class and announced, "Every cadet training to become a pilot must jump from a plane with a parachute." Of course this made logical sense, but nonetheless we shifted uncomfortably in our chairs, looking at each other with sidelong glances and nervousness at the idea of jumping from a plane. The only exception was one of our fellow cadets who'd been a professional skydiver before joining the Air Force. She smiled and rested easy in her chair.

The following day we took a course on the procedure of jumping from a plane and deploying a parachute. We learned stance and positioning and how to tackle various scenarios. As we did so, I couldn't help but ask myself, *Is this reality? Will I really be jumping out of a plane?* To quell my unease I spent the afternoon going over all of the procedures, again and again.

On the day of the jump, I wondered if bad weather would postpone our jump. Maybe it would have to happen at a later time. But we woke to dazzling skies and perfect conditions. There were no clouds or wind, nothing to smudge the canvas of an ideal day, and I tempered my disappointment that the jump wouldn't be postponed with the joy of feeling the sun on my face.

As we approached the airfield, I felt a new stirring inside of me regarding the impending jump. It wasn't fear or excitement, but curiosity. I was all too aware that this moment in time would stay with me for the rest of my life.

The airplane, an AN-2, was a monstrosity compared to our training plane and not my favorite aircraft. We called it "the closet" as it was boxy and looked like it served little purpose beyond storing jumpers and their gear, as opposed to some of the more graceful planes to which we'd been introduced. I sat next to my best friend, and we smiled down our fears and apprehensions. I tried to hold on to the feeling of curiosity instead.

It came time to put on our parachutes, a smaller, reserve parachute in front, and the main, larger parachute in back. The main parachute was so heavy that I was unable to maneuver it myself and had to have help from the instructors. We were to be taken up in groups of four, and I was part of the first group. *Would I be able to walk with the weight on my back?*

The sky was so blue and the day almost too quiet as I lumbered my way onto the plane, trying to keep from toppling over under all of my gear. My fellow cadets and I were quieter than usual, each focused on keeping panic at bay and talking ourselves out of the fear of what was to come.

Before I knew it, I was sitting on the plane's long interior bench. My hands were ice cold, but I was lucid and kept a calm face. Perhaps too calm, as a colleague nodded in my direction and asked, "Aren't you nervous?"

"Of course," I mumbled. I said nothing more, unable to put into words the mix of fear and determination I felt. How could I explain that though I was deathly afraid, I also wanted to jump?

As the airplane climbed and reached the right altitude for our jump, a red light came on, which was the signal for us to get ready. The other three girls and I stood and shuffled our way toward the door. When the instructor opened the door, I felt as if the abyss of blue sky was swallowing the plane. I no longer felt my heart beating, it had stopped along with time and space.

The red light dimmed and the green light lit up. The first girl jumped, then the second. The third girl, who was in line before me, began to panic.

"I don't want to jump," she shouted at the instructor above the roar of the plane. "I don't want to jump!"

He began shouting back and then physically pushed her out the door. The skirmish took up valuable time and the plane was no longer in the correct position. The instructor closed the door and told me to stand by until the plane could circle back to the right spot. When it did and the door opened again, there would be no one before me in line; I would be first to jump.

The red light came back on. I stood up. The main parachute weighed painfully on my back. I couldn't feel my legs anymore and briefly questioned where they were, or if I even still had legs. The instructor opened the door and I stared at it, wondering how stupid I had to have been to agree to jump out of a plane into nothingness. When I flew in a plane, I sat in a chair, I had something underneath to support me. Now I'd have nothing.

I looked at the wing of the airplane, using it as an anchor to focus on and refusing to look down at the emptiness that awaited me. Then the green light came on with a loud sound. I placed my hands on the door frame, holding tight. I heard the command, *"Jump!"*

I closed my eyes and threw myself into the abyss, facing the front of the plane and bringing my arms and legs into a ball, unified and together like the world around me. I was conscious only of falling in that moment. I counted to five and pulled the cord to open the parachute. I felt like a cat's play toy, a ball of yarn being pushed and pulled in all directions.

The time passed quickly but seemed like an eternity. A few seconds felt like years. I looked up to check if the parachute opened properly, opening my eyes for the first time since I jumped. I looked up and saw that everything was fine. Then I looked down. My first reaction was, *My God, it's so beautiful!* The world from the sky exceeded my expectations. I had never seen anything so wonderful, the sky and earth with me floating in between. I felt free at the high altitude and as if I'd never reach the earth. I felt, simply, happy.

Slowly I maneuvered myself to land where the other parachutists were. I heard the instructor shout, *"The legs!"* and took the position for landing. Though I landed smoothly, the weight of the secondary parachute dragged me down and I fell on my back. Through fits of laughter I announced, "I would like to jump one more time!"

8

NO DAY SO CLEAR BUT HATH DARK CLOUDS

In the summer of 1987, the female cadets began our first training on the helicopter. We trained at the Boboc aviation base while Adi, in his third year of college, was flying the L-39 Albatros jet. Flying a helicopter has been likened to maintaining balance while standing on a ball. It requires a lot of coordination, but I was getting good at it.

The morning of that Saturday was quiet. The sun was shining high in the sky as the airfield came to life, breaking the silence of the day. General Constantin Mereu, the head of the Air Force College, was flying helicopters with us that morning. The grassy airfield for helicopter training was within walking distance of the college, while the male cadets took a short bus ride to the jet runway on the other side of the hangars.

While I was flying my helicopter, my mind was on Adi, who on that day would fly his first solo flight. He'd be alone in the L-39 Albatros jet. I was proud of him, as he was one of only two cadets in his class that were yet permitted to do their first solo flights. My gaze kept turning in the direction of the jet runway, hoping to catch sight of him landing. Of course, it was too far to actually distinguish one plane from another, but that didn't keep me from imagining which plane might be his.

My thoughts were interrupted by an urgent conversation on the radio.

"Mr. Commander, a jet airplane is not answering on the radio. His last report was ten minutes ago."

"What jet was it?"

"It was a solo one."

My heart stopped beating. I couldn't feel my pulse. All physical sensations ceased, save for a tightening in my throat. There were only two solo jet pilots flying that day, and one of them was the man with whom I wanted to spend the rest of my life. A pilot not answering on the radio is often the first indication of a crash.

The commander's voice came over the radio again. "Stop flying," he said. "Everybody lands."

I landed my helicopter without even knowing what I was doing, my limbs somehow going through the motions without my conscious effort. I searched the faces on land for answers. "Who is the missing pilot?" I screamed to everyone and no one in particular. "Who is it?" I demanded.

My desperate pleas for information were met with a constant chorus of "I don't know." No one knew who was missing. Frantic with worry, I ran toward the jet airfield. It was all I could think to do, just run and keep running. I had to find Adi and not think about what might have happened to the missing jet.

Helicopters began taking flight again, sent out to search for the missing aircraft. The distance to the jet airfield seemed endless. A rumbling from behind me signaled an approaching car, but I paid it no attention as I continued my sprint. The car passed by me, a staff vehicle heading to the airfield to deliver lunches to the cadets. Later I would learn that when they saw me running, word began to spread that it was Adi who was missing.

I ran that day not only for Adi, but for myself. We were one and the same. In essence, I was running for my life. When I finally reached the airfield, the second solo jet was coming in for landing. *It has to be him. Please, let it be him. I cannot live without him. He is my life.* The jet came to a stop and the pilot emerged. A moment later Adi was walking toward me with a smile on his face. My distress was clearly evident as his smile fell away.

"What happened? What's wrong?" he asked.

All I could say was, "I thought..." before my tears took my breath away.

Adi took me in his arms and said, "No, Smighi is missing."

We hugged each other, maybe the sweetest hug we ever had. I cried in happiness that I'd found my love, my life, and I cried in sadness for our colleague who was still missing.

Helicopters searched for the missing pilot and plane all day, while ground crews scoured the earth. There were no witnesses, except for a lone farmer who saw the plane flying at a very low altitude. He did not, however, see any sign of the plane crashing, and we took solace in that. The absence of a crash site was suspicious, but also brought us a measure of peace.

Indeed, the next day the Turkish government confirmed that a Romanian jet had landed in their country. Smighi asked the Turkish government for help in claiming political asylum and relocating to the United States. In time they agreed, helping Smighi with his plea for asylum and returning the plane to Romania, without its pilot.

On campus, no one dared talk openly about the courage it must have taken Smighi, along with no small amount of luck. He had found his freedom. He was no longer caged by our country and its leaders.

Romania's Communist government was, of course, not pleased. General Vasilea Milea, the Minister of National Defense, came to our college to investigate how it had been possible for a pilot cadet to evade detection and successfully defect. Smighi had flown lower than 150 meters from Boboc, through Bulgaria, and then to Turkey. A remarkable accomplishment, not least of all because he'd done so during his first-ever solo flight in the L-39 plane. His phenomenal undertaking was also a slap in the face of the Communist regime.

At the time, Adi was part of a committee whose job it was to recruit his colleagues into the Communist Party. He was called into an office to be questioned by General Milea and General Mereu about Smighi. "Did you notice anything in his behavior lately?" they asked. "Had you seen him studying the geography of the surrounding areas?" Adi answered that he had not. "And why wasn't Smighi a member of the Communist Party?"

Adi could only answer truthfully: "I take people in alphabetical order," he explained. "And Smighi starts with 'S'." Adi didn't care about the committee. He participated only because he was obligated to do so; hence, the decision to carry out his duties in alphabetical order.

General Milea's face began turning red in a mixture of disbelief and anger. Our general fidgeted and fretted about the consequences of Smighi's defection. He was an incredible commander, and an amazing pilot who was fully dedicated to the Air Force College, its cadets, and his passion and dedication to flying.

General Milea moved forward with his questioning. General Mereu never mentioned it again. Just as Adi never told a soul that Smighi had indeed asked for his help with geography and questions about how to fly low to avoid detection. Of course it crossed Adi's mind why his fellow cadet might be asking such questions, but Adi never said a word about it. He helped Smighi when he could, and the things that didn't need to be said were left unspoken.

To remain in the military and to graduate from the college, all students had to become members of the Communist Party. I simply wanted to get it over with, while Adi evaded it for as long as he could. Eventually, in his second year, he became a member. It was a package deal and there was no escaping it. Some students took their membership in the party very seriously while for others, like Adi, it was simply a necessary step if he wanted to pursue his dream of flying. When it came down to it, though, Adi's spirit was always free.

Once he was almost dismissed from military high school for listening to Radio Free Europe. He didn't hide his listening or his tiny radio that sat next to him on the window ledge, which was daring for him to do. One of Adi's colleagues must have been an informant and told the security officers. Adi was in trouble and his father had to go to the military high school. Adi was interrogated but somehow managed to stay in school. He had a secret desire to leave Romania as soon as he could, but his love for flying took him on the military path that he silently detested.

There are little clues in the pictures we have from those times about how Adi really felt. In almost every photo, you can tell he feels choked in the military uniform. His cap is always off to one side, slightly askew. Or the buttons on his military jacket are undone, almost haphazardly so. He carried the wish to leave Romania inside of him, but he also saw that I was tied to our land, nor did I have any idea what might exist beyond our borders. I dared not think of it.

Even in the Communist system, being in the military was a privilege, and one that came with the necessity of joining the party. Some members cared, others only pretended to, just to get by and make it through college. We were always aware of the danger that there might be a whistle-blower among us, and because of that we refrained from sharing our true feelings, or anything that could potentially harm us. It was often a simple guess to wonder who the informants might be, but when rumors circulated, you could never be sure who to trust. Information came sporadically, through unidentified and invisible sources. It felt, at times, like fighting phantoms. Even your best friend might turn out to be your worst enemy, but there was never any proof. Only your word against that of an invisible accuser and the swirling rumors. In that society, we were guilty until proven otherwise, but there was no jury to hear your case, so it might end up simply buried and forgotten.

After Smighi's defection, the administration limited the amount of fuel allowed in the training jets. Only enough was permitted for thirty minutes of flight time, just enough to take off, do a small bit of training, and then land. Nothing more, to limit any further possibilities of escape.

The Saturday of Smighi's escape was significant for many reasons. Smighi had found his freedom. But it was also significant to Adi and me, as we learned just how much we needed each other. When I remember the fear I felt that day, the fear of losing him, I can't think of it without my eyes filling with tears. My heart instantly aches, the same way it did then. God was with us that day, and I hope God will be with us forever.

9

HOME IS WHERE THE HEART IS

Visits to my parents' home grew shorter and shorter as time went on. When we were given two weeks of vacation, I'd tell my parents that I'd only been given one, and that Adi and I were splitting the time off between their house and Adi's parents' house. As such, we'd end up spending only three days with my parents. While they thought we had the same amount of time with Adi's parents, in reality we'd be with them a full week and a half.

It wasn't simply because we were more comfortable at Adi's house, but also that we were growing more uncomfortable at my house. My father, normally a kind man, was increasingly lost to his drinking. My mother was unceasing in her judgement of my relationship with Adi. And my brothers were involved in their own lives and interests. This perfect storm led to me feeling like a stranger in the very house in which I was raised.

The atmosphere at Adi's house was quite different. We'd play with his younger sister, pick blueberries in the summer, and go sledding on a hill near his house in the winter. Our time there was enjoyable, despite the night when we went sledding too fast and the sleigh tipped over, hitting Adi in the head. On the walk back he kept asking me what had happened, over and over again, despite my repeated answers. I thought he was joking but soon realized he wasn't. The next morning he was fine, though he never regained his memory of sledding with me that night or hitting his head as a result of it.

At school, Nelu would sometimes come visit on the weekends,

jumping the fence to do so since he wasn't supposed to be there. Adi would give him a blue aviation uniform to wear so that Nelu's presence could go undetected. Nelu and I had always been close, and having both him and Adi there created some of my happiest college memories.

When we got the chance, Adi and I would take trips to Bucharest where Nelu was attending the Military Academy. Though officers patrolled his dormitory, we'd sneak in and stay overnight. It was tricky and there were many times when we were almost caught, but the idea of staying in a hotel was both unthinkable and unattainable, so we took the risk. Nelu had a new girlfriend, Sorina, who was studying to be a teacher and lived on the outskirts of Bucharest. They met when her school invited Nelu's class at the Military Academy to a party. Sorina had two sisters and a very close-knit family, and we had wonderful times visiting them often.

On one occasion, after Adi and Nelu drank too much wine, they suddenly realized that French was their forte. They talked in what seemed like fluent French deep into the night, until morning came, when the French disappeared and gave way to sickness and hangover. The next day, they didn't remember speaking French at all.

Sorina's home quickly became our refuge. There we felt warm, welcomed, and loved. I remember feeling puzzled when Sorina's mom, whom we called Mamaia, would help her daughters with outfits or do their nails. I'd been raised with only negative comments from my mother when it came to my appearance, and was never encouraged with anything to do with fashion or makeup. As a teenager, my mother once scolded me for wearing makeup. I was shocked and confused, later realizing that I had a smudge of soot on my face after rubbing my eye. My mother interpreted that transference of pollution as the transgression of a teenager.

When it came to Sorina, her sisters, and us, Mamaia was always cheerful and ready to help, relentlessly cooking and setting more dishes out on the table for us. "Just have a good time," she would say.

Once a year we had to go to Bucharest for medical checkups. We would always manage to go together. One year Adi's sinuses were hurting him badly and we worried about how that might affect his performance in the barometric chamber exams. The pressure would surely only increase his sinus pain. As the time led up to the exams, I was so worried about Adi that I forgot that I had to take the exam as well. The next thing I knew, the nurses were trying to wake me up and I was covered in vomit. I failed the exam, but still all I could think about was Adi. I was sent to a variety of doctors to figure out what was wrong with me and why I'd failed the test. No one could find anything wrong with me, so the internal medicine doctor told me to take a week of medical leave. "Go home, rest, and eat properly," he instructed. "Then come back and take the test again." Of course, instead of going home, I went to Adi's father's house. When I returned to college, I took the test and passed without issue. I'd simply been overstressed the first time.

Outside of school, my mother and I clashed when it came to how I should spend my time. Specifically, she thought a lot less of it should be spent with Adi. The fact that I loved him and wanted to spend all of my time with him fell on deaf ears. While many people's relationships operate with time spent apart, I always knew that Adi and I were different. Our relationship flourished when we were together all the time. That's what worked for us. We were always there for each other. Whenever my mother heard that I'd again been spending time with Adi and at his father's house, she'd again voice her disapproval. When I pressed her on the issue, she said, "People are talking." I was both shocked and hurt to learn that small town gossip was more important to my mother than her daughter's happiness. I felt powerless and sadness embraced my body. Why would I stop seeing Adi so much when he was the one who truly cared for me, protected me, and was there for me when I needed him? I wasn't giving up, but neither was my mother. Finally, I asked, "If we got engaged, then would you be fine with me seeing Adi and visiting him at his house?"

She looked me in the eyes and, after a moment, said, "Yes."

I turned on my heel and stormed out of the house, to where Adi was waiting for me, worried about my latest argument with my mother. I walked directly to him and said, "Can we get engaged? The sooner the better, please. My mom won't leave me alone and let me be with you if we don't get engaged."

He looked at me calmly, hugged me and kissed my sadness away. "Of course we can," he said. "Let's talk to my dad about what we need to do and then we'll just do it."

Adi's father took the news about our engagement fine, though much later in life I learned that he took Adi aside and encouraged him to seriously consider if he was doing the right thing. "Just look at her mother," he advised. "The apple doesn't fall far from the tree, so just make sure you're making the right choice." Adi replied that he was confident in his decision and knew that I resembled my father more than my mother. Adi adored my father, despite never knowing him in his prime, before his drinking truly took hold. And that was that, we were engaged.

When we returned home from summer break, we had a small feast in honor of our engagement. Adi's parents were there and his father had helped get a ring. I was to choose my engagement present, between a necklace and a ring. I chose the ring. It was customary to then name the godparents, a Greek Orthodox tradition in which an older married couple become spiritual parents and mentors to the younger bride and groom. On such short notice, we asked our neighbors and they kindly accepted.

Friends and family gave us presents like glasses, blankets, and coffee sets, things to use in starting our life together. Material items were rare and expensive in Communist Romania, so every little thing counted for something and was treasured. Because we were still in college, I packed everything away for safekeeping in a little room at my parents' house. Over the next few years, whenever I was home I'd notice things that I was sure had been gifted to Adi and me for our engagement.

"Isn't that wine glass set mine?" I'd say, pointing to glasses in the cabinet that hadn't been there before.

"No," my mother would quickly answer. "I bought those."

"Isn't this the blanket I was given when Adi and I got engaged?" I'd ask, motioning to a new, warm winter blanket on my parents' bed.

"No," she'd reply again. "That's the blanket I bought."

By the time Adi and I would finally move into our first rented apartment, all of the gifts were decimated. There was no point in arguing or fighting over it, but I was nevertheless hurt that she was still pushing against my happiness instead of helping me start a new life. As time went by, being at home would only grow more painful. The rift between my mother and me widened, eventually bleeding into my relationships with my younger brothers as well, causing greater distance between myself and Doru and Marius.

Adi and I were engaged during my three remaining years at the Air Force College. We would have married sooner, but the college prohibited it. The school took all of the entering cadets' national identification cards, which we would have needed to wed. The administration's stance was that they didn't want to be responsible for us if a cadet became pregnant. They couldn't allow any interruptions in a cadet's four years of training. If students weren't married and got pregnant, that was their responsibility, meaning they would be dismissed from college with no opportunity to return and resume studies. Like most cadets in relationships, Adi and I knew that we needed to behave and wait until after graduation to get married. That was standard practice, though one of my fellow cadets managed to get married one year before graduating. This surprised us all and we weren't sure how the couple had done it. Word got around that the cadet in question had a boyfriend in the Army. He was graduating a year before us and it was important for him to get assigned to a military unit where she would be working upon her graduation. Only marriage guaranteed it.

I was never one to be easily impressed or look up to role models. I was strong from childhood and with Adi grew even stronger. But every now and then someone stands out to me, and I greatly admired a particular couple that I met during my college years. Every fall we were sent to the kolkhoz to help with the corn harvest. One fall was particularly tough, as I was assigned to help out in the accounting office. A captain worked as the primary accountant, along with a secretary, who was a civilian hire. I worked mostly with the captain, but the secretary was very friendly and I grew attached to her during my time there. She was petite with brown eyes, short hair neatly done, and always nicely dressed. It was a change to see someone in civilian clothes instead of in a uniform every day.

At the end of my two weeks, I learned by mistake that the captain and secretary were married. I couldn't believe it. Nothing they did or said gave them away. Puzzled and impressed, I took the opportunity in private to ask the captain how they managed to do it. Smiling and speaking softly, the captain said, "When we get off the bus in the morning, we don't talk about home or chores or our kids. We work. Then when we get on the bus to go back home, we don't talk about work. We talk about home."

I was impressed by how they managed this, and recognized that the balance and separation were how they kept their marriage alive and happy. Everyone must find their own way and figure out what works best for them. For Adi and me, what worked best was being together and sharing everything. We had a closeness not always present in relationships, a fact of which I was reminded often, not only by my mother's disapproval, but also when the other Air Force girls would advise me not to share everything with Adi and be so honest with him.

In August of 1988, Adi graduated. We dreaded the day, because it meant we would have to be apart. I still had a year left of college while Adi was assigned to Bacau to train on the MiG-21 jet. We knew that the only chance for us to be together after I graduated was for both of us to be assigned to units near Constanta, where I would fly helicopters at Tuzla and Adi would fly jets at M. Kogalniceanu. Both aviation units were within a commutable distance of Constanta, a beautiful town on the shores of the Black Sea. We didn't know if it would be possible, since both were highly sought-after posts. Every pilot dreamed of flying the newest MiG jets at M. Kogalniceanu so competition was fierce, but it was all we could hope for.

On the morning of August 23, the day of Adi's graduation, we both overslept and were late. Adi didn't care much for formalities, but his presence was mandatory, and I wanted to be there because I liked the event, and moreover, I was proud of him. I hurried to ready myself in a special dress I'd bought just for the occasion.

When Adi rushed late to the event, Captain Eminescu Coserea spotted him and asked where he'd been. Before Adi could answer, the captain said, "Never mind, I already know. I bet you were with Rodica."

The first time I saw Captain Coserea after starting college myself, I recognized him immediately from the TIBCO exhibition one year earlier in Bucharest. He was the captain whom I'd approached to ask if the first year cadets were there. He was the one who'd given me hope that day that I might see Adi. When I saw him that first time, I felt like I'd known him forever. His calm, warm face conveyed the reassurance that I'd so desperately sought that day.

After a brief summer vacation, I returned to finish my senior year at the Air Force College while Adi started his training on the

MiG-21 at Bacau. Luckily there was an express train that ran from Bacau to Buzau. Because Adi was staying in a military hotel and I was still in the dormitory apartments, it was more convenient for me to visit him than vice versa.

Bacau was an unexpectedly nice city. On top of its charm, Adi now had a salary and we could afford to dine on a romantic meal at a restaurant. I felt extremely spoiled to be able to do so, have a nice meal in a restaurant with Adi, especially after so many years of scrimping by.

Most of the time I would visit on Saturday afternoon and then return to Air Force College on Sunday. I'd travel to Bacau by myself and Adi would always be there, waiting for me at the train station. When it was time for me to leave, Adi would often insist on accompanying me, saying that he wasn't comfortable with me traveling by myself so late. He didn't want me walking the last two kilometers by myself at night. It didn't matter that there were always other cadets around or that 8:00 p.m. wasn't really that late or that the area was fairly safe. Adi would board the express train with me to Buzau, then wait with me for the local train to take us to Boboc and then walk those last two kilometers with me. Once I was safely inside the building, he'd begin the return journey: walking two kilometers, waiting for the local train, then switching to the express train. He'd arrive back to his room late when he should have been taking the time to rest. He made that journey with me many times. When I could tell he was truly exhausted, I'd try to convince him to let me go on my own, but he wouldn't have it, as apparently I wasn't very convincing. So I gave up trying and just focused on enjoying our time together. I could have taken Adi's actions as a sign of jealousy. Did he not trust me? In truth, jealousy and mistrust had nothing to do with it. Adi was simply protective of me and always made sure that my well-being was a priority, even when it meant sacrificing a bit of his own.

10

THE HEART WANTS WHAT IT WANTS

The first female pilots graduating class of the Romanian Air Force did well. Really well. We were disciplined, determined to fly, and not only did we graduate, we excelled. Upon graduation, our class had the highest grades in the college, as well as the senior with the highest grades overall. When the administration learned that the rightful valedictorian was a woman, they were less than pleased. As such, they decided to have one male and one female valedictorian. Those of us who knew the full story felt that she deserved to go to the podium alone.

We graduated at the rank of lieutenant on August 23, 1989, after receiving the military pilot's license. We made history. I remember the general saying, "Too bad the *Aviation History* just came out. When Volume 2 is written, it will start with you."

After graduation, I went home to prepare for our September 2 wedding. It was slated to happen in my parents' garden and, as was customary, in a large tent constructed by the community. Everyone would contribute with wood for the benches, tablecloths, and beautifully decorated rugs for the walls of the tent. Then the children of part of the town would decorate the tent with *hartie creponata*, decorative Romanian crepe paper. If you were lucky and lived on a quiet back street, you could put your tent in the street. Otherwise, the tent always went over the garden, and you'd pray that it wouldn't rain and turn the soil into mud.

If we'd strictly followed tradition, we would have married at Adi's house. Since he'd left home at fourteen, he didn't feel it was right and wanted instead for his brothers to have the opportunity to be the first to marry there. If we had married at Adi's house, his parents would have paid for all of it. Instead, we were to be married at my parents' house, but my parents also agreed to pay for all of it. When it came down to it, Adi and I didn't necessarily want a wedding so much as we just wanted to be married, but my father told me that he wanted to see his only daughter have a wedding, so we agreed.

Just as with the tradition of the community helping set up the tent for the wedding, Romanian communities also came together to bring gifts that would help the young couple start their new life. Gifts were often money, but also they helped with bringing in chickens, flour, eggs, sugar, and other staples so that the expense would not be too great on the hosting household. The parents would often discuss with the couple ahead of time if a certain amount of money given to the couple was to be used to pay back the wedding expenses. Since my parents had agreed to cover the wedding, this wasn't an issue.

Without many of the wedding expenses to worry about, we had a beautiful lace wedding dress made for me in Bacau. Adi saved up for it and I felt as if my prince had given me a gift, lifting me up from Cinderella's despair.

When we got home, the whole house was preparing for the upcoming event. People bustled in and out of the house, bringing goods and supplies and gifts. Outside, people were putting together the tent, and everyone worked in the communal spirit of volunteerism. Then it started raining. It rained the whole week prior to the wedding, and it just wouldn't stop. The tent floor became muddy, people wore boots and sometimes became mired in the muck. Despite the chaos, only Adi and I seemed worried about it. The others continued working happily to finish on time. Tables and chairs were made, rugs were hung, and the kids laughed and listened to music while hanging the colorful crepe paper decorations, stretching from one side of the tent, to the middle, and then on to the other side. Slowly, the muddy tent turned into a beautiful setting for a wedding. There were open places left for the dance floor and the musicians. But all I could see was mud, mud, and more mud. Adi recognized the worry in my face. He took my hand and said, "I will do something about this," glancing at the muddy floor. "I can't see you dancing in the mud in that beautiful dress." And with that, he left for town.

He returned later that day. It was Friday and the wedding was scheduled for Saturday. He announced that he'd secured the city banquet hall for our wedding and that everything needed to be moved there. And that's exactly what we did. The food, decorations, tables and chairs, everything was relocated. To this day I still don't know how he managed to secure the room. He knew no one at city hall, I can't remember any other wedding taking place there, and above all it was the day before the wedding. We would have to pay for the room, but still, it was unheard of.

It was a huge room with ample space for all of the attendees. Adi and I only had a few people we'd invited, including Adi's dear friend from the Air Force whom I got to know quite well when Adi was in Bacau since they shared a hotel room, with my mother doing most of the invitations to friends and family. Nelu was getting married the following week. He'd wed Sorina in June in Bucharest, at a wedding hosted by her parents. My parents were hosting a second ceremony for the newlyweds at our home, so many distant relatives came to stay for both my wedding and Nelu's celebration. Other friends could only come for one of the two weddings, and I found out later that my mother encouraged all of her closest friends to come to my brother's wedding. She made no effort to hide the fact that she loved him more, and she was far more invested in making sure that his wedding was a success than mine. That's not to say she wanted my wedding to fail or didn't work hard in the preparations, but this was yet another detail in our relationship that let me know how she truly felt.

On Saturday morning, we went to city hall to officially get married. The rain stopped and September 2, 1989, turned out to be a beautiful, sunny day. Our parents and a few close relatives and our best friends joined us at the city hall ceremony, where we wore our Air Force dress blues. After, we went home to get ready for the wedding and I realized I'd forgotten to pick up my bridal bouquet. Adi's brother graciously offered to pick it up for me, and then we went to the banquet hall.

The wedding was a whirlwind and everyone had fun, laughing, dancing, and celebrating. It was a success that could not be derailed by minor details like mud or forgotten flowers. And then Adi and I were summoned to a back room. We were there, along with our parents and god-parents, to receive the money that had been collected to give to us as a wedding gift. We were all there to witness it being counted, which totalled 37,000 lei. I remember the sum, thinking it was a nice amount with which to start our new life, far away from our families.

Then my mother started talking about the money we needed to pay to cover the wedding expenses. It was as if, standing there in my beautiful, tailor-made wedding dress, someone poured a bucket of cold water over my head. I looked to my father, but he kept his mouth closed, not uttering a word of protest. Everyone else in the room was silent, too. The only sound was my mother's continual assertion that the expense was too hard on them and how we should give them at least 15,000 of our wedding gift to cover the expenses. I protested. This was both unexpected and unfair. But then Adi pulled me to the side. "Just let her have the money," he said. "We'll manage just fine like we always have. Let's not give any more energy to this conversation." I gave in and agreed.

We returned to our guests who were dancing and having a good time, but with the clock creeping towards morning and the news we'd just received, we couldn't bring ourselves to enjoy it anymore. Near 4:00 a.m., as the first guests were getting close to leaving themselves, we just left, walking all the way home alone. When we arrived, my maternal grandmother was there. She looked surprised to see us. "Why are you alone?" she asked. "Where is everyone else and why are you back so early?" Through tears of frustration, and while already packing up our things, I explained what had happened with the money we were to be gifted. "Oh, I can't believe it," my grandmother said. "I'll talk to her when she gets home. How could she do this to you?" I didn't have an answer.

By 5:30 a.m. we'd finished packing, and said goodbye to my grandmother along with apologies for leaving so early for the train station. As we left, she stood in the doorway with her hands crossed and sadness in her eyes. She stared in disbelief at how we were leaving my parents' home and our wedding—what was supposed to be such a joyous day. We simply needed to get as far away as possible from what had caused us so much pain.

At 6:00 a.m., we sat on a wooden bench in the empty train station. Our train wasn't due for another two and a half hours, but we preferred the station to staying even one more minute in my parents' house. The train ride back to Bacau was long and painful. Adi got physically sick from being so upset, while my tears kept coming, wishing I'd never listened to my dad and agreed to the wedding. I knew he meant well and wanted us to have an unforgettable day, but it turned out to be unforgettable for the wrong reasons.

The next few days, our honeymoon, was spent in a hotel trying to regain our strength and getting Adi well again.

Twenty-five years later, on our silver wedding anniversary, we'd have the party we always wanted. On that night we were smiling and our hearts were filled with happiness. It was an opportunity to reflect on all that we'd been through and accomplished together, and it was truly a night to remember all for the right reasons.

Before graduation, I received the assignment I'd hoped for, the military unit in Tuzla, Constanta County. Our commanders had done well by us, doing their best to match our assignments with our wishes. Though Adi was still in Bacau, we had hopes that he could join me soon. There were four of us girls all assigned to the same unit, and one of them was from Constanta County. She was gracious enough to offer me a place to stay until we had our situation sorted, and I was grateful for a cozy place to stay while I was far away from Adi. I set my sights on the day we'd be reunited.

II

EVERY DAY IS A NEW BEGINNING

As a young lieutenant I started my career at the Military Unit 02010 Tuzla, which was to be my workplace for the next four years. The missions there involved the IAR-316B Alouette and IAR-330H Puma helicopters. The primary role of the aircraft regiment was to remain prepared for combat in support of ground troops, though the helicopters were also used to reach offshore drilling rigs, conduct coastal research and agricultural missions, and aid in rescues from sinking ships and natural disasters.

My colleagues, who had arrived a few days before me, told me that the parachutists were arriving at the military unit and preparing to jump. As helicopter pilots, parachuting wasn't a mandatory exercise for us, but we were given the choice to do so. All of the girls chose to jump.

Our first jump was over land and I felt the same butterflies in my stomach as I had when first jumping out of a plane in college. After that, we were asked if we wanted to jump over the water. The unit was close to the Black Sea and jumping over water was a routine part of training for the jet pilots. When asked if we wanted to do the Black Sea jump, we all answered, "Sure."

The colonel, head of the parachute team then asked, "Do you know how to swim?"

My three colleagues all answered in the affirmative. I said, "No." It turned out I was the only one who didn't know how to swim. The near-drowning incident in the canal during childhood had maintained a fear of water in me and I'd never tried to learn to swim in the intervening years. And yet there I was, agreeing to jump from a plane and parachute into the Black Sea.

"Are you sure?" asked the colonel.

"Yes," I confirmed.

"Okay, I'll make sure you each jump with a professional diver, just in case you need help."

I quickly learned that the procedure for jumping over a body of water was different and far more challenging than jumping over land. When you reached the water, you needed to be free of parachutes to keep them from falling over you and dragging you down. This meant untying two parachutes, detaching them from my gear, and inflating the life vest, all in under a minute's time. I was less concerned with finding myself surrounded by water in the sea, miles away from shore, and more worried about how I'd manage to get rid of the parachutes before reaching the water.

Leading up to the jump, I practiced over and over. *Untie the big buckle first, then take the belt...* I continually replayed the instructor's words, trying to perfectly commit them to memory. My will to jump outweighed my fear of water, though that fear was real and continues to this day.

When the day of the jump arrived, the colonel kept his word and paired each of us with a diver from the Diving Ships Division. It was a beautiful sunny day and I felt the push and pull of mixed emotions. Normally I was cool under pressure, but how would I manage all the steps that needed to happen in "under a minute"?

We donned our parachutes and boarded the plane. In the plane I sat on a bench next to my assigned diver. "I'll help you out," he said. "Don't worry." He was a short, muscular man who radiated confidence. I couldn't help but wonder, though, how he'd manage to stay at the same altitude as me after we jumped. He was heavier and would just fly right past me, leaving me unattended in the sky. He must have read my mind, because he added, "I'll jump after you, so I'll be at the same height with you when it's most critical to judge if you're doing all the steps." That was somewhat reassuring, though I was still preoccupied with remembering the order of events and how to make sure I could untie the parachutes and get free of them. That was my main focus, and I replayed the steps many times in my mind, forgetting about the diver and the sea and all that worried me.

My thoughts were interrupted by the colonel's voice over the radio. He called to the crew of the waiting boat far below us. "Be ready and be careful. The lieutenant who doesn't know how to swim is going to jump now. Get ready."

There was no time to stop and take a moment of joy in admiring the blue sea and skies. The expanse of sea struck me as immense, colliding with the skyline, leaving an undefined line of where one ended and the other began. I stood and headed toward the open door, my heart shrinking in my chest. Then, as I took the position, my fears disappeared and I jumped. I counted and pulled the cord. Looking at the parachute above me, I could see that it was wide open, as it should be. I could move on to the next step.

I started to inflate my life vest, first by taking the knob out from the left side and blowing into it. I closed the valve and then repeated the process to inflate the right side. Then I began to untie the first belt from my front parachute. Still falling through the sky, I felt that my life vest wasn't inflated enough and went through the process of inflating it again, first on the left side and then on the right. In hindsight I could see that this wasn't necessary and that the vest would have kept me afloat without inflating it twice.

Suddenly I noticed my diver, quickly passing by me. He was obviously trying to communicate with me as he rocketed toward the sea, but I had no idea what he was trying to say. At that point I couldn't worry about him. I looked again at the parachute above me to confirm that it was still wide open. Then I unlocked the main belt. It felt as if I was falling out of my gear, but they'd warned us ahead of time of that sensation. I untied the reserve parachute, pulled it up and passed it through the main strings before pushing it back over my head. Then I pulled the main belt under me as much as I could and held on tight to the strings. I was ready for impact into the water. For the first time I looked at the sea in all its beauty and blueness. It seemed so far away still, but it was difficult to estimate the altitude without landmarks by which to judge the distance. Nevertheless, I was ready. When I felt that only a few meters remained between me and the sea, I let the parachute go to head alone into the water. For a second, panic snuck into my mind and body. *Was I, who didn't know how to swim, actually jumping into the deep and limitless sea?*

It was too late to hold onto panic. As my legs reached the water, I felt the sea start swallowing my body, dragging me into its infinity. I closed my eyes, held my breath, and hoped that the uncharted area of sea would have mercy on me and let me go, instead of dragging me down into uncomfortable depths. *How deep will I go?*, I wondered. I had never been so far under water.

Not only was I unable to swim, but I'd never even dipped my toes into the Black Sea before. My first experience with it was jumping from a plane, discarding my parachute, and fully submerging myself into the depths. The sea surrounded me with its arms, making me wonder if I'd ever get out.

My thoughts didn't have a chance to continue down that path, as the sea hurtled me up to its surface with immense force and I could breathe again. I opened my eyes to enjoy the blue of the sea and sky. Floating in that moment, I felt an unexpected peace. I saw the boat rushing toward me to pull me from the water, but hoped it wouldn't arrive too soon, to experience that peace within the sea and myself a minute longer.

As the boat neared, I was surprised to see my assigned diver in the vessel, instead of near me in the water. The boat had passed by him first on its way to me. With a smile on his face, he pulled me into the boat and said, "If you would have inflated that vest anymore, I think it would have exploded. I was trying to tell you it was sufficiently inflated, but I guess you couldn't hear me." It turns out that communicating while hurtling through the sky past one another is not terribly effective.

We headed to shore where a helicopter was waiting to fly us back to the military base. It was the first time in my life I'd seen a beach. Dripping wet, with a radiant face and feeling indescribable joy, I boarded the helicopter saying, "I want to jump one more time!" And lucky me, my wish was granted.

12

NO GAIN WITHOUT PAIN

In November of 1989 I watched President Nicolae Ceauşescu address the nation for the Communist Party's 14th Congress. It was mandatory that we view the speech, and we crowded close together around a small television in the military unit. I remember clearly because his speech, for the first time, made me doubt that Adi and I would live to see a better Romania. Ceauşescu said that, as a generation, we were sacrificing ourselves, not for the sake of our children, but for our children's children and generations after. It was depressing enough to hear that we shouldn't be hopeful of seeing better days within our lifetime, but the sadness was compounded with the message that our children would endure lives with the same hardships. They'd have to wait in long lines for the necessities of life, endless waiting for simplicities like eggs and oil. Was this all we could hope for in life? That perhaps our great-grandchildren might have less difficulties?

Despite the bleak future, we managed to be in a relatively good position during that time, doing well for a young couple just out of college. The Air Force paid us well and kept us fed. At work we were given three meals a day, and for days off we were given food rations like meat, eggs and sugar. Sometimes we accumulated an excess of food and I'd offer it to our neighbor. She was always appreciative as she had four children to feed. We also had hopes of saving money and buying a car.

Adi had left Bacau having finished the one-year training on the MiG-21; he was then assigned to Borcea. It was closer to Constanta, where I lived in our rented apartment. He wasn't yet assigned to M. Kogalniceanu. The competition was fierce because it was the best Romanian Air Force base equipped with the best jets, the MiG-23 and MiG-29. Every pilot's dream was to fly them.

I'd always imagined that our efforts were in pursuit of a better life for our children. I couldn't imagine them still having to suffer the same hardships as my generation, which was an uncomfortable possibility the president's speech had implanted in my mind.

By the winter of 1989, things were different. On December 17, riots broke out in Timisoara. We weren't aware of them at first, though on that evening while Adi visited me at Constanta, we found out that we'd been called for duty on fight alarm. All of us—the entire Romanian military was called into active duty.

Adi left for Borcea while I embarked for Tuzla, with no idea what to expect or why there was an emergency. Our Tuzla Helicopter Regiment 59th was led by Lieutenant-Colonel Ioan Tarina. General Vasile Milea gave the order for *Radu cel Frumos* which implemented the battle plan for all military units to prepare for combat.

Though it was mid-December, the weather was unseasonably warm, as if nature was telling us to fill the streets, raise our voices, and fight for freedom. It's hard to imagine how some of us need to voice our desire for freedom and feel trapped in an oppressive system with no hope of escape, while others thrived on that very system, and still others remained completely at peace with it. I don't pretend that I easily fit into that first group. My desire for a better life was tempered by my patriotism. I felt a duty to my country. I wasn't interested in what happened beyond our borders, or maybe the poverty in which I was raised, where all energy was invested in making ends meet, kept me from even thinking about it. But I was proud of my country and everything that came with it. As conditions deteriorated and I saw the hardships around me, I thought it was normal. I hadn't been exposed to any other way of life, so there was nothing with which to compare it.

By December 21st we'd been in the military unit for a few days, not permitted to go home, but also not told why. That day we were told to report to the flight room because the president had a televised message for us. All the pilots gathered in the flight room around a small television in the corner. We were ready for President Ceaușescu's speech and what was supposed to be a rally in support of his regime and policy. Sitting there like schoolchildren in class, we pretended not to be bored by the lecture. It was our duty to watch Nicolae Ceaușescu brag and brainwash us. Inside though, I felt my love of flying and my duty to my country far outweighed the unspeakable behavior of his and the conditions we were forced to deal with every day.

Suddenly, there was movement in the crowd and people began to raise their voices. You could see a small wave of movement, and then another, until the whole crowd turned into a giant, unstoppable sea of unrest. Would the people begin marching? It was unreal and surreal, like watching your soul leave your body. Even in our dreams we were afraid to hope for such a thing. Hope mixed with fear that the people raising their voices would stop. The boredom that weighed in the room a moment before gave way to our unspoken desire to keep watching. We were afraid to talk about what we were seeing. And then, the transmission stopped. The broadcast was interrupted at 12:54 p.m. We were no longer witness to what was happening, no longer a part of hope for change.

The television screen went white, with black dots. No one in the room moved, we waited for something to happen, afraid to give voice to our inner thoughts. Afraid to look one another in the eye. Afraid to hope. Afraid that the protesting crowd we'd seen moments before were being shot down, and that our hopes would be shot down with them.

We had questions we didn't dare ask. We were isolated from any news about what direction the events were taking, or where our country was going. It was a matter of life and death; people were dying in their fight to overturn Communism and its president.

The awkward silence was broken by an order. We were told to get our AK-47s and prepare to fight. It was a day when I witnessed senior military officials break down in tears. The conflicting emotions, torn between being faithful to the system, for we'd taken an oath to support and fight for that system no matter what, but what of the population we were supposed to suppress? What if the President called on us to kill our own people? That was the question, without an answer, on everyone's mind.

The magnitude of the situation didn't hit me immediately. I was more concerned about Adi, miles away, and if I'd ever see him again. I wasn't preoccupied with my own security, the fight against Communism, or the prospect of a civil war and fighting our own people, our own blood. What hurt my heart that day was that when we went to the basement where the ammunition and weapons were and took them to prepare for civil war, I couldn't be with my loved one. I didn't mind the call to fight…if I had Adi by my side. At that moment my tears didn't fall because I might have to shoot innocent people in the name of a lost and unwanted cause, those tears would come later in the streets as gunfire surrounded me. My initial tears were for the fear of losing the person I loved and cared about the most. He was my home, my country, my world.

We were in the basement picking up the weapons and ammunition, which I can still feel in my hands. Cold, unwanted, harmful, hateful, repulsive. No one would get to return home that day, or the next day, or the day after that. We had no change of clothes and only cold water in the showers, but who needs a change of clothes or hot shower when the future was in shambles, gray and unknown? The needs of our souls transcended the basic needs of living. The aspirations of our souls led in one direction:

freedom.

We were isolated from news, our only information came in the form of orders from our commanders. The days were unbearable to get through. We grew tired, somber, and anxious. The men became haggard and unshaven. Most of us suffered through sleepless nights. We were bunked down, at war and yet fighting no one.

We later learned that unknown sources created false targets that invaded the skies on December 21st and 22nd. They were visible on our radars, so from the ground the army fired rockets at aircraft that didn't actually exist. We heard conflicting information of whom we may be fighting, and the waiting was torture. They were days of uncertainty and contradictory orders. Everyone's face conveyed worry, but not panic. We had joined the military to fight enemies, not our own people. The lack of information and the absence of a true enemy made the waiting all the more somber.

News of Ceaușescu's fall eventually came on television from the national headquarters in Bucharest. A group of revolutionaries went to the television studio and asked to talk to the Romanian people. They began televising live updates and called themselves "The Romanian Revolution Live." It was a surreal and unforgettable scene, like nothing we'd ever witnessed. It was the deterioration of Communism and the building of our hopes for a better country.

Ceaușescu's capture wasn't the end of the bloodshed or worry. Rumors spread of hidden terrorists or Ceaușescu's secret army that would fight to the end. The country existed in a vacuum of power with no clear direction of where to head next. The television gave us confused and conflicting messages, none of which came with any verifiable proof. In the midst of it all, we sheltered the hope that our country was headed for democracy, that Ceaușescu wouldn't return. When we heard that Elena and Nicolae Ceaușescu had been captured, we received the news with open arms. It was as if we'd been collectively holding our breath, and now we could breathe again.

Bucharest became the epicenter of the revolution, and the confusion that went along with it. While I was in alarm mode at the Tuzla Aviation Unit, and Adi was at Borcea, Nelu was in his last year as a cadet at Bucharest's Military Academy. He later recalled, with sadness and a trembling voice, how they got involved after the Ceaușescus left Bucharest in a helicopter from the top of a building on December 22. They were gathered at the Academy and told that they needed to protect the Minister of National Defense from terrorists, though those same terrorists were never seen or proved to exist. They were told to take ammunition and board the buses. Nelu was in the second bus, wondering what the purpose of it all was and how it would play out. There was little information, and therefore little decision-making at the Army level. No one knew which side they were on. In the midst of it came the news that General Vasile Milea had committed suicide. That was horrible enough in itself, compounded by the fact that he was the head of the Army and could have used his power to do something, to provide direction.

The buses headed through streets full of protesters, demanding freedom. As the buses pulled in front of the building of the Minister of National Defense, the students on the first bus got off. Nelu watched in horror as they were rained on by a cloud of bullets. Nelu couldn't believe it, that they were being shot at by people they had been called to protect. They were being fired on by our own Army, the Ministerul Apararii Nationale soldiers and officers. No one bothered to tell them that the cadets were on their way to offer support, and Nelu's colleagues were killed, having been mistaken for terrorists.

The tumultuousness and uncertainty of the times continued in my world as well, as the next morning, on Saturday, December 23, our unit received a call from the military aviation commander to execute a reconnaissance mission for enemy aircraft. They were given a route to fly that included an offshore drilling platform in the Black Sea. Three Puma helicopters, fully equipped for combat, roared to life. The sound of the engines, once a welcome sound that brought joy, seemed now to be the roar of death looming around us. It disturbed the day, the sky, and took our own peace with it.

We watched as the helicopters disappeared in the mist, hoping for their safe return. When they got back, they described flying over the sea at low altitude, the cold air sweeping through the helicopters, chilling their bodies and souls. They had machine guns and flew with the doors open, ready for combat, ready to fight an enemy that never materialized. They found nothing at their targeted locations in the sea and had to go to M. Kogalniceanu to refuel. There they were shot at, having been mistaken for the enemy themselves. Everyone felt the stress and uncertainty of exchanging fire with invisible enemies, and so ended up exchanging fire with themselves. The helicopter managed to land and be recognized before anyone was hurt. We listened to their story in disbelief and relief that they'd actually made it back alive. By this time the president and his wife, having fled Bucharest, had been captured. So why did the fighting and gunfire continue? Why were lives lost?

13

ALL'S FAIR IN LOVE AND WAR

An unsettling panic embraced my body. I kept calling, but no one would answer. Time and time again I dialed the number, just hoping that this time it might be different. My heart leapt when instead of endless ringing, someone finally picked up the other end of the line. But my heart dropped again when the person on the phone said that they had no information for me. They didn't know anything; they couldn't help. When I called again, I was told to stop calling, stop inquiring about Lieutenant Ponici's well-being.

It was a few days after the start of the Romanian Revolution in December of 1989. Military units were on alert and on duty around the clock. Airplanes were taking off on search missions and I couldn't shake the feeling that something bad had happened to Adi, something no one was willing to tell me.

Those few days were unbelievably warm, almost like summer. By December 24 we'd been in the military unit for almost a week without warm water or a change of clothing. We took turns on duty and when we were off, struggled to keep warm and get sleep on whatever we could in the chilly building. Most nights were sleepless, not only because the building was cold, but more so because it was such a time of uncertainty and stress.

That morning, the airfield was busy getting underway. Two helicopters, Puma-82 and Puma-89, were ready for combat and preparing for an aerial search mission. The orders were that they were not to be intercepted, which meant no radio communications and flying at low altitudes, to look for an unidentified helicopter about eighty kilometers west of the airport. We were all together in the flight planning room as the four pilots of the two helicopters prepared for their mission. The room was furnished like a classroom, with benches for seating and a large blackboard that sat behind a desk at the front. There was an air of gravity that hung heavy in the room, as if the rest of us could feel the bravery emanating off of the pilots. It took no small amount of courage to go fly when military units all around us were shooting, though no one knew the exact reality of what was happening, or even who the enemy was. The nature of a revolution comes with many unknowns.

Two days prior, Elena and Nicolae Ceaușescu had departed Bucharest, but we were still shrouded in confusion about our mission, our enemies, and our allies. In the night you could hear shooting and see the sky light up. Confusion led to fear, not only for our own safety, but at the prospect that we might be asked to fire on our own people. That was the greatest fear.

Major Paul Constantinescu was in the flight control tower, on duty as the deputy commander. He was a humble, soft-spoken man with a passion for flying and a significant amount of experience to back it up. It was easy to see that he enjoyed aviation, though in those days the fatigue and uncertainty seeped even onto Major Constantinescu's face.

The crew made their way to the helicopters and began their preflight routine. After getting Major Constantinescu's approval, they took off in formation and quickly flew out of sight. Without radio contact, we'd have no information until their return.

I was in the flight planning room with colleagues and there was palpable tension when we got the news: one of the helicopters had returned, but the other had been shot down. Four people had perished, the two pilots along with two mechanics who'd been on board. The information was unreal, inconceivable.

The room took on an eerie silence, so much so that I felt I could hear our hearts beating out of our chests. One of the returning pilots told us that they'd heard a loud noise and had tried to reach the other crew. When no one answered, they flew back and saw the other helicopter on the ground, crushed in a pile of metal and smoke, before fire erupted, embracing the wreck in a deadly shroud that ensured there were no survivors. The crew of the second helicopter looked on helplessly. There was nothing that could be saved from the crash, and when the ammunition on board started to explode, they were forced to turn back and return to the base. Before they made it back, our flight control tower made contact to check on both helicopters. Puma-82 responded, but Puma-89 did not. One of 82's pilots said simply, "Puma-89 is gone." The silence at such news was paralyzing, until one of our colleagues broke the stillness by approaching the blackboard and writing the four names of our deceased crewmates on it and drawing a rectangle around those names. It was so finite. We kept a further minute of silence to honor their memory and bravery.

The reality of the revolution hit us hard, especially the fact that there was no visible enemy. There were no facts, only rumors circulating that did little other than foster confusion. We were fighting invisible enemies and, most likely, shooting at each other, just as the PUMA was likely shot down by our own army.

After the loss of the Puma crew, I was more determined than ever to hear from Adi. The following morning, on December 25, the commander allowed the women pilots temporary leave to go home, change clothes, and refresh ourselves to return the following day. Though our male colleagues had taken pity on us and given us the alarm cell in which to sleep, while they slept on floors or wherever they could, we still had no extra clothes or hot water with which to shower, despite the fact that we were our own aviation unit.

Though we were eager for a break, we left the military unit that day with heavy hearts over the loss of the Puma crew. The four of us women hitched a ride home, through town where the streets were nearly abandoned, but the sounds of gunfire rang out sporadically.

After I reached home, I showered and tried to relax, but couldn't stop thinking about how I might learn news of Adi's well-being. Frustrated by my inability to eat or sleep, I left the rented apartment and began walking toward the train station. I heard gunfire along the way, but couldn't tell where it was coming from. I felt vulnerable in my civilian clothing, without a weapon and without Adi's protection. My desire to learn of Adi's safety was stronger than my concern for my own safety, so I continued on. I reached the train station and hopped on the first available train that would take me in Adi's direction. He was stationed at Military Unit Borcea, about 100 kilometers away.

I took the train to the Fetesti station. I'd never been there before and didn't know where the Army Aviation Unit was located, but I approached the bus drivers that were stationed outside of the train depot. One of them told me that while none of the buses went to the Army Unit, he could drop me off at an intersection just a few kilometers from Borcea. I'd have to make the last leg of the journey on foot. I felt a surge of gratitude. When he dropped me off on what looked like a road to nowhere, he pointed in one direction and said, "Keep going straight and you'll reach the Army Aviation Unit."

I started walking, remarking to myself what an amazing day it was, still sunny and warm on Christmas Day. I wore a light blouse as it felt like summer. At one point I passed by a few tiny houses. Gypsy children jumped around in circles by the side of the road, exuding joy and singing *"Ole, ole, ole, ole, Ceaușescu nu mai e."* Their song translated to "Ceaușescu doesn't exist anymore," and I wondered if they knew anything of the ongoing revolution or if they were just repeating something they'd heard from adults. Regardless, there was a sense of liberation and relief knowing that Ceaușescu was no longer in power. As I passed the children, I caught myself smiling at their innocence, purity, and passion.

I reached the post and realized I was in luck. The guard on duty was a former Air Force College colleague of Adi's and he recognized me immediately. "You came to see Adrian," he said. "That's so nice of you. How have you been?"

I was overjoyed to see a friendly face with no hint of worry. His words and smile brought me happiness and the knowledge that Adi was safe. Otherwise, he'd surely have broken any bad news to me, I reasoned. We chatted briefly before he directed me to proceed farther to the second checkpoint, where I was told to wait. I felt the fatigue of my long and arduous journey until finally, there was Adi coming toward me! Relief washed over me, though Adi wasn't smiling. His face registered fear and shock. He was upset that I'd put myself in danger to get to him. He knew how unsafe my journey must have been and was further concerned by what he perceived to be the suicidal notion of me making the return trip that afternoon. Instead, he made a few phone calls and took me to a nearby apartment building that was home to military families. A mother and daughter took me in, welcoming me to stay overnight, for which I was very appreciative. As night fell, the exhaustion and stress of the day took their toll, seeping into every bone in my body. Adi had to return to work, and my gracious hosts fed me dinner. Before we said goodnight on that Christmas evening, we turned on the television.

Three days prior, the revolutionaries had caught Elena and Nicolae Ceaușescu. The leader of the Romanian Communist Party and his wife had already been tried and sentenced to death. We were shocked to learn that the execution would take place immediately and also be televised.

Nicolae Ceaușescu sang what sounded like "The Internationale" as he was led to the firing squad wall, while Elena Ceaușescu screamed and cursed at her captors. As soon as the couple was in place against the wall, a wave of what seemed like hundreds of bullets washed over them and their bodies fell. Though we questioned why they had been executed so fast without a proper trial, we also felt relief and hope that we might now attain a sense of peace. Romanians had waited too long for the end of the Ceaușescu regime to feel any sort of guilt. The overwhelming hunger of the previous twenty years demanded their execution.

As I went to sleep that night, I wondered how I'd get back to my Military Aviation Unit. I'd felt invincible in my journey to find Adi. Nothing could have stopped me, even if I'd had to walk all the way to find him. Going back was a different story and the dangerous reality of my situation settled in. As well, I only had twenty-four more hours off duty. Or so I thought.

The next morning Adi picked me up from the apartment. We thanked the wonderful hosts and walked to the main road to hitch a ride back to Fetesti, which was the closest town. We reached the train station quickly and without incident, but then I began to experience an unsettling feeling. I told Adi that I needed to call one of my colleagues back in my unit to make sure everything was okay back on our side of the revolution. I couldn't reach anyone. No one answered at home. My disquiet grew as I began to fear the worst. I called directly to the Air Force base and asked to speak to one of the girls. One of them answered the phone. "Where are you?" she asked with an unmistakable note of panic in her voice. "Last night they called us to come back in but we couldn't reach you. The commanders are worried because they couldn't get in touch with you either."

My heart sank with the realization that I was potentially a deserter from the military. I told Adi what had happened. He insisted on returning with me to my Air Force base. He wanted to make sure I made it back safe, but also to do whatever he could to protect me.

"That's all we need," I protested. "Two deserters in the family."

I couldn't bear the thought of him getting in trouble as well. With a heavy heart he reluctantly agreed to let me return on my own.

On the way back I stopped at home to change clothes and then caught a bus to the Air Force base. While walking from the main road to the Military Unit, my thoughts were consumed by what might lay in my future. I kept thinking about prison or detention. After all, I was missing for more than twenty-four hours, which was desertion.

At the checkpoint, one of my colleagues greeted me with a smile, which put me at ease. If he wasn't arresting me on the spot, then maybe news of my situation wasn't yet widespread. I took that as a good sign.

I walked in the building and the flight escadrille captain looked at me angrily, ordering me to get dressed in my flight uniform and report to Major Constantinescu as soon as possible. I entered the control tower with big, determined steps, hoping they might mask the shrinking of my heart. There he was, Major Paul Constantinescu, coming toward me with blue eyes that managed to be both soft and intense. His face registered worry, but only for a split second until it turned calm, and then almost happy to see me.

"You went to see Adrian, didn't you?" he asked. I nodded my head as my eyes filled with warm tears. "Is he safe?" his calm voice continued.

"Yes," I whispered, tears now rolling down my cheeks.

"Good," he nodded. "Now get your gun and get in position. No one needs to know about this further."

I've never forgotten the kindness that Major Constantinescu showed Adi and me on that day. Everyone knew how Adi and I felt about each other, that our marriage and bond was as strong as anything, but I never would have guessed that in the midst of a revolution, at the height of nerve-wracking uncertainty, someone would bet on their confidence in our relationship. In essence, he trusted in our relationship, though it put him at risk by not reporting my absence to the authorities, as the law prescribed. His faith in me, knowing that I was seeking answers and Adi's safety, as opposed to just going missing or deserting my post, will forever be appreciated. Commanders were known to react in panic at the time, caught in the untenable position of having to choose between the Romanian president and the Romanian people. In those difficult times, the major had somehow managed to keep his judgement in check, his demeanor upbeat, and his heart open.

Later that week, my colleagues and I went to Constanta to attend the funeral of the Puma crew. Each of the four crew members received a postmortem advance in rank and were buried with military honors. The funeral was quiet, the silence ending only when the sound of shots rang out. We knew that our duty at that moment was to protect those present and not expose them to further danger. As such, the service ended quickly. We couldn't even grieve in peace because we were still at war. With ourselves.

14

WHERE THERE IS LIFE, THERE IS HOPE

The morning my father died, I slept in late. I woke at 11:00 a.m. Those days I often slept in late, and that Saturday, the first day of February in 1992, was no exception. I was eight months pregnant with our first child and already on maternity leave from my Air Force job. Adi had managed to get reassigned at M. Kogalniceanu and had completed his training for the MiG-23. It had been over two years since the Romanian Revolution. Hope for a better life was still alive, though Adi and I tried to remain realistic and grounded.

I was at home the day that two apartments were assigned to our regiment and offered to the pilots. No one wanted them. The first apartment was in a region mostly populated by ranks lower than officers, and the second apartment had a nice central location, but was in deplorable condition. When I found this out, Adi and I went to the central military office and asked to see the apartments. We picked the first one and didn't mind the location at all. We were happy to move in and be able to call the place home, decorating simply and with comfortable furniture we bought from the previous owner. Material things were never our focus, instead we concentrated on our relationship and made the effort to enjoy our lives together and have as much fun as we could. We felt good about starting a family and decided to have a child.

My pregnancy was relatively easy. I thought about sharing the news with my parents, but then changed my mind. Adi and I were so happy and I didn't want anything to spoil it. Early in my pregnancy, in September of 1991, we were on our way to visiting my parents and I told Adi that I didn't want to share the news with my mother, which of course meant that my father wouldn't know, either. "She won't be happy for us," I said. "And I can't bear that, so I would rather just not say anything." Adi supported me in whichever way I chose to handle it. When I saw my dad, I felt sorry for denying him the happy news. I knew how happy it would make him, so I changed my mind and decided to tell them after all. We were in the backyard, my father sat by the sidewalk that ran in between the main house and the smaller one. He looked thoughtful, with his hand on his forehead, and I imagined he was dreaming about how to finish his dream house. Even though he wasn't making progress on the house anymore, I knew he still kept thinking about it. My mom was standing nearby, so I took advantage of the moment and broke the news.

"Mom, Dad, I'm pregnant. We're going to have a child," I said.

My mother looked at me, murmured, "Fine," and walked away.

My father stood up to hug me and began crying tears of joy. "Now I'll have two grandkids to play with," he said. "This is so great!" Our nephew, Nelu's son, was already eight months old.

I hugged him back tightly, unaware that it would be the last time I would do so.

I went to find Adi, who somehow managed to sneak out and avoid any type of confrontation. When I saw him, I sadly said, "It was exactly like I thought it would be. Daddy was so happy and she just ignored it. But I feel better now that I've told them. At least Daddy knows and is looking forward to it."

In general, I didn't keep in touch with my family or brothers very often, nor did they keep in touch with me. Because of this, no one told me how sick my father was. Heavy drinking had taken a toll on his body. In January my mother called to let me know that my father was in the hospital; he'd been spitting up blood. In my innocence, I thought little of it, for nothing bad could happen to my father.

After waking in the late morning, on that fateful Saturday in early February, I grabbed an apple. Adi sat next to me, uncharacteristically quiet. Too quiet. He waited until I finished my apple, and then said the dreadful words, "Your father passed away."

I couldn't comprehend what those words meant. I tried to imagine my dad dead, but I couldn't. It wasn't conceivable, so I asked what exactly he meant. The answer wasn't what I was looking for because it was the same information, repeated.

"Your dad died."

I couldn't believe it.

It couldn't be true.

Adi explained that my mom had called that morning. She wanted him to make the decision about telling me and, if he did tell me right away, it was up to me whether or not to attend the funeral. Considering my late stage pregnancy, she said everyone would understand if I did not.

"Understand" is a mighty word. She never understood my dad. I always thought that for every brick he put up, she took two down.

There was no question of not attending the funeral. The twenty-four-hour trip was nothing compared to the loss I'd just endured. That Saturday night we boarded a train bound for the other side of the country. It was a long, sleepless night.

The next day, on Sunday, we stopped at my uncle's home in a nearby town. There we found out that the funeral was the following day. I'd thought the funeral was on Tuesday, not Monday. We had no time to spare. We left in a hurry for my hometown.

Every second seemed irreversible. I know they are anyway, but those moments hurt, being conscious of the way the seconds ticked by, being away from my dad.

At home I found my mother in a constant state of tears, crying all the time. I couldn't understand why. Was it because people were watching? Was it because people were judging? Was it for the sake of tradition? Where had she been while he was alive? When he needed her to listen, to stand by his side, to support him?

We kept the body at home until it was time to take him to the cemetery for the funeral. When I approached my father's body, I removed the veil covering his face. I wanted to see him one more time. It was my last chance to look at my father's face. Old ladies bustled around, trying to get me out of the room and cover him up again. I kept returning. I wanted to be there, by his side. They kept saying that I was pregnant and it was against custom to stay with a dead body. But to me this was not a dead body, this was my dear daddy they were talking about. And as far as going against custom, can someone really explain what custom means to a heartbroken and suffering daughter? They tied a red string around one of my fingers telling me that way I could stay. The string was a superstition, meant to keep anything bad from happening to my baby in the presence of death.

I don't know who was there or what they did that Sunday night. My mother came into the room a few times, wailing loudly. Each time I took her back out of the room. She was disturbing my peace and my dad's peace, nor did I believe her grief.

I stayed there with my dad, by his side. His hands were bruised black and blue from all the intravenous needles during his time in the hospital. That was it. That was all. That was the end. I wondered if I should feel happy that he was at peace, far away from her, far away from suffering.

That night I couldn't remember a single thing my father had ever done wrong.

Not the nights he drunkenly kept us awake while I begged him to let us sleep because we had school the next day.

Not the days he'd promise me he'd go to work, and then when I'd leave for school he'd start drinking again and skip work.

Not the time he beat my mom, or the time when I broke his finger trying to save her.

Not the endless promises he made so many times, promises that things would get better, but they only ever got worse.

I remembered only the good times, when we were younger and he played with us, when he stepped in and saved me from my mother's anger, when he dreamed about rebuilding the house, and when he'd say, "My darling children, what else can I do for you?"

When we were young, my father smiled. He was smart, witty, and always ready with a joke. Those good times were, unfortunately, short-lived. Before I left home at eighteen, it was hard to see what was wrong, and I blamed him. I never talked to him about his drinking issues or not keeping promises or beating my mom or not providing us with a stable environment. He commanded respect, and he knew what he was doing wrong. He was vocal about it when he wasn't drinking and he always promised that he'd get better, that he was getting things under control and would follow up on his promises to stop drinking. He would manage to stop drinking, but only briefly before he'd fall back into his old routine. Over time, the periods of him not working grew longer and longer. After I left home and had my own relationship, I started to blame my mom for not staying by his side more and fighting with him and not against him. The truth is always in the middle and I am sure both could have done more, for their relationship and for their children.

I don't remember sleeping that night. I stayed dutifully next to him, watching him for the last time. The funeral service was held the next day in our backyard. My mother, brothers, relatives and neighbors were there around the casket, with Adi by my side, holding my hand and understanding my pain. Adi loved my dad. He once mused what the world would be like if people would be only half the man my dad was. He was kind, loyal, and loved his family to the end.

In many ways I felt that he'd sacrificed his life for us. My father knew where he was heading and how unhappy he was becoming. At one point he had the chance to leave us. He wanted to start his life from the beginning, and give up the life he'd created as well as the drinking. But that meant giving up not only on our mom, but giving up on us children as well. And that was unbearable to him. He would have never done that. He stayed by us to provide for us and slowly went down a destructive path with no way to return. His decision to stay killed him slowly and surely as his relationship with my mom deteriorated.

"Look up, Rodica," Adi said.

I lifted my chin to the cloudy skies, unseasonably warm for early February. Directly above the coffin, ten white doves circled at a break in the clouds. I watched, mesmerized by their presence at that moment, right there and then.

After the backyard funeral service, we began walking to the cemetery. I was offered a ride in someone's car, but politely refused. I wanted to walk behind the coffin. A few miles wouldn't harm me or the baby, though at the cemetery the old ladies once again intervened, telling me I couldn't go next to the coffin as it was lowered into the ground. Superstitions again. I guess the red string they'd tied around my finger had lost its power to protect me. I no longer had the energy to fight back and resigned myself to sitting nearby.

When we returned from the cemetery, snow began to fall, quietly and beautifully and—I couldn't help but think—like my father's soul. No one dared talk badly about him, at least not in my presence. Years would pass before I'd convince Nelu of the harm my mother caused to our family. I love her for being my mother and raising me, but it's difficult to forget what she'd done to me and my dad.

After the funeral, Adi and I went to my father-in-law's home in a different town where I planned to have the baby. He'd left Adi's mom and started a new life in Sebes with his girlfriend Olga, and I planned on staying with them for a month while awaiting the birth of our child.

Tears for my father kept coming. I cried quietly every day, trying not to for the sake of the baby, trying to keep the sadness at bay, but it was so hard to manage. Then one night I had a dream. I stood in the road in front of our house and my dad was walking towards me. He was shrouded in fog, but I could still see it was him.

"Rodica," he asked, "why do you keep crying? Why can't you let me go? You are keeping me from moving on."

"It's too hard," I answered, "because I never got the chance to say goodbye."

He looked at me for a moment before replying, "If I came back one more time and hugged you, would you let me go?"

I said yes and he did, he hugged me right there in my dream. It was the goodbye that I didn't have a chance to say when he was still alive.

The next day, I felt better. I woke without tears, at peace with myself and my dad.

On the evening of February 22, my contractions began. Adi had left to return to our town, and I asked my father-in-law to tell him to come back. As Adi made the return trip, I waded through a night of contractions. My father-in-law and Olga kept asking if they should take me to the hospital, but I said no. I knew it was too early for them to do anything, and in any case I wanted to forgo medications. By morning, the contractions were very close and at 5:00 a.m. I asked Olga to help me wash up before we left for the hospital.

They hailed a cab and took me to the hospital, where the doctor confirmed that I was close and encouraged me to walk around, but I couldn't. It took all my strength just to lay down in bed and try to control my breathing. Other pregnant women in the room with me began chatting amongst themselves. One spoke of miscarriages and how another woman had recently lost her baby. In between contractions, I whispered if they could please stop talking about such things since I was, at that moment, in labor. Grave silence filled the room before one of the women apologized, saying that they hadn't known I was in labor because I was so quiet. I thought about telling them that I was trying to conserve my energy, but even voicing that would have used up energy. I kept quiet all the way to the end.

After my little baby was born, I didn't want anyone touching me. I felt that I was done and didn't want any further outside intervention. I wasn't happy about them having to stitch me up, but once I held my baby in my arms, all of the pain was forgotten. His little face, outstretched arms, mouth searching for food, everything that made up my son in that moment, was worth all of my efforts and more.

The next morning, I found myself in a room with four other women who had also recently given birth. The doctor came in to visit and ask us questions, including what names we had thought about for our babies. When it was my turn, I answered, "Riky."

"What is that?" the doctor asked, "A dog name?"

I was puzzled and saddened that the doctor would say something like that. We knew "Riky" wasn't a Romanian name, but nevertheless we liked it.

Towards evening, I felt both fatigued and fragile from having given birth and the stay in the hospital. I called Adi to come as soon as he could in a taxi, no easy feat because taxis were scarce. I walked slowly down the hallway to meet him; at that time men were not allowed in the birthing or recovery rooms. With milk-soaked pajamas from my leaking breasts, I looked and felt a mess. As soon as I saw Adi, I burst into tears and, between breaths, told him of the doctor's callous dismissal of our chosen name.

"Have whatever name you want," Adi said softly, "just don't be upset, it breaks my heart."

"Olga likes the name 'Alin'," I said. "Maybe we'll go with Alin."

"Sure," he said.

"But we only want one name to avoid the confusion of having two," I said.

"It's fine if it's only Alin," he replied, desperately searching for a smile on my teary face.

The following morning a hospital administrator came to register the baby's name. Hearing my story, a lady next to me said, "Why would you care what the doctor says? Just have both names if you really like Riky."

And that was that. He became Riky to us and Alin to the rest of the world. Two names, what we'd hoped to avoid in the first place.

Having Riky in our lives renewed our hope for a brighter future. We took our baby home and revelled in the pride of having our own life and our own family for which to care. We settled into our new roles of parenthood well and for a short but blissful time, I was able to care for my son without any worries of work. That is, until exam time. Every year, a commission came to our military unit to issue the pilots annual licensing exams. That year I was exempt, as I was home on maternity leave with Riky. Despite my exemption, I desperately wanted to take the test with my colleagues. If I didn't, I'd have to take it at a later date in a different town, one not of my choosing. I much preferred to take the regularly scheduled exam than later have to deal with the hassle of travel. I would just have to go back to work for a few days, and this would save us headaches down the road. But who would care for Riky?

Out of desperation I called my mom and asked her to come for a week to stay with us and help care for her grandson. She agreed. She came with Nelu and his family. It was summer, and as we lived close to the Black Sea, it was an opportunity for them to take a road trip and enjoy the beach.

They arrived in time for the weekend. Around noon on Saturday

I was in the bedroom with my mom and took a moment to express my happiness.

"I'm so glad you're staying with us for the week," I said. "I don't know how we'd manage without your help."

"I can't stay," she responded curtly. "I leave tomorrow with Nelu. I am going back with him."

My breath caught in my throat before I managed to speak. "What do you mean you're going back?" I asked with incredulity. "You came to help me out and stay. You agreed."

"Yes, I did, but I don't want to go back by train. It's a hassle. I want to go back with Nelu by car."

My mother had always been eager to display her preference for Nelu, especially when I was in times of need. Her callousness was unfortunate not only because she was my mother, and the grandmother of my son, but also because her behavior inadvertently caused Nelu and me to drift apart over the years. Nelu, who'd been my rock in childhood, now felt as if he existed on the other side of a great divide, in the middle of which was our mother.

I stumbled out of the bedroom and directly into Adi, who had overhead the unfortunate conversation. Adi was always close by at such moments, to catch my unhappiness and bring me back to life. When I saw his face I could read that he heard everything. I collapsed in his arms and murmured, "She wants to go back tomorrow. What will we do Monday? What about the whole week? How will we manage? I need to take my exams."

"Let her go back," he said. "Please let her go back. I am begging her to go back. We'll manage...we'll ask our neighbor Angela. Between her and me we'll manage to take care of Riky while you go to work."

My mom emerged from the bedroom, taken aback by his words.

"How he can say that I can just go back home?" she demanded. Apparently she wanted to leave, but also wanted to be indispensable.

Calmly, I turned to her and said, "It wasn't him, remember? It was you that wanted to go back. He just agreed with you. And yes, you are going back tomorrow, just like you wanted. We'll be fine."

The next day she packed and left. No remorse to be seen. No apology to be heard. She left nothing behind but her absence. The hollowness of my relationship with my mom only intensified the pain of losing my dad and his unconditional, unfailing love.

15

A WOMAN'S PLACE IS IN THE KITCHEN

Life taught me that I am strong and have the power to stand up for my rights. But I also recognize that Adi was instrumental in showing me my self-worth and bringing my inner strength to the surface. He helped me see that I can do anything I put my mind to, whether that was succeeding in the military, breaking through stereotypes, or learning to care for our child.

Adi had a talent for protecting me and caring for me, while at the same time helping me grow stronger. In my early days of motherhood, Adi would take Riky to the living room to care for him so that I could catch up on much needed sleep. We always shared the chores, the good and the bad. We didn't consciously plan it this way, our teamwork just came naturally in our relationship. "Give and take" was our secret to a successful marriage. You can't always take, for if you do then soon enough you'll reach the bottom and there will be nothing left to take.

Much later, after fate would intervene and separate us against our will for months on end, I would argue that maybe Adi had shielded me too much in his desire to protect and care for me. He replied, "But just look how you managed by yourself after I left. How you stood up for yourself and our child. How you took care of Riky. I wasn't there to protect you and you did amazing!" He was right. I couldn't argue with that.

Part of Adi's protectiveness of me was likely to shield me from a culture in which men prevailed; the inequality between men and women was blatant. My pilot colleagues later told me stories of how hard it had been for them to survive in the aviation units. For the four years I worked there, however, I wasn't overly exposed to it, with one exception before I left. My limited exposure to the gender inequities stemmed from the fact that I didn't work enough to get to the point of competing for promotions with my male counterparts, so the unfairness didn't always reveal itself. While in the Air Force College I felt protected that we women were part of a pioneering event in the whole of Romanian history. We knew we were special. Our accomplishments were previously unheard of, but of course ingrained societal habits like discrimination and misogyny don't die easily, and this was clearly reflected once we started working in the real world.

There were times when I had to stand up for myself, such as when I got my driver's license. It was initially Adi's idea. "It doesn't hurt having it," he suggested, and I agreed. Eventually we planned to buy a car, the Romanian dream. We even calculated how much we'd have to pay per month and for how long. (It was a long, long time). In the end we bought a cheaper car, a Trabant, and so we were able to get it earlier than planned. Many officers wouldn't drive a Trabant since it was cheaper and associated with a lesser status. Adi didn't care about such things. He was practical and wanted the convenience of a car sooner rather than later. As well, gas was both sparse and expensive. The Trabant would take any type of gas and Adi always managed to find some.

We took driving lessons through the military school; it was the fastest way to get a license and also free for us. The downside was that the license for driving a car went along with the license for driving a military truck. So there I was learning to drive in a huge truck. Adi didn't see it as an issue and even then I didn't give it much thought. *Adi al meu* (My Adi) was the best and taught me well. I was his wife, best friend, and partner. He never put me down and encouraged me to think for myself. He trusted me completely, just as I trusted him completely.

ENOUGH LOVE

Without realizing it, in Air Force college I often brought "My Adi" into conversations, along with his opinions and ideas. I did this once in a classroom discussion about flying. A colleague looked at me and asked, "And is this what *Your Adi* thinks, or you?" The girls laughed. It wasn't a compliment but a dig. I grew quiet, knowing there was no use in trying to explain how our relationship worked, and most of all, that it worked for us. Adi was smart and proved time and time again to be right. He knew aviation and its theory inside and out, often better than the teachers. So who were they to laugh at me, at him, at our relationship? Years later, when we got together in Bucharest, my closest dear friend said, "You remember how the girls used to laugh at your relationship? Look around now at where they are with their relationships, years later. Never married or divorced or stuck in a marriage that's on the rocks. You've had the last laugh without ever needing to say a word."

It was no surprise that I believed Adi when he told me I could learn to drive a big truck in my early twenties. Adi accompanied me on every lesson. I felt bad for the soldier whose job it was to teach me to drive and pass my practical test. He was nervous enough teaching a lady pilot lieutenant how to drive. Having my husband there watching only made him more anxious. He was either shy of giving me instructions or not very good at his job, because at one point Adi just told him to get out of the truck so that he could teach me how to drive himself. The instructor was hesitant exiting the vehicle, especially because of an abrupt edge on one side of the parking lot that he feared we might plummet over. But Adi wasn't worried a bit.

"Don't worry about it," he scolded the nervous instructor. "I know what I'm doing and my wife will learn faster if I teach her."

The soldier exited the truck and Adi took his place. As always, he knew how to push me and allow me to make mistakes, instead of always stepping in to correct them. It was his way of telling me that he trusted me, but he'd also always be there to help if I needed it.

A flash of fear swept through me when the truck neared the edge of the drop-off, but I stopped it safely and, as time went on, realized I was getting better at driving the truck. After just a few days of practicing, Adi felt I was ready, and the soldier gave his blessing for me to take the road test.

It was a rainy day with clouds playing in the sky, accompanied by the unmistakable sounds of thunder, foreshadowing the pouring rains that would follow. With the onslaught of rain, I thought the road test might be cancelled, but it wasn't. I was nervous. My adrenaline was running high, but out of fear instead of excitement. I was nervous about performing well, as I wanted to make Adi and myself proud. The test would be difficult enough as it is, but on top of that I was the only woman taking the test. If I failed, I felt it would be doubly embarrassing.

I easily passed the road test for a passenger car, then found myself in a bus with all of the others who needed to take the road test for the truck, which drove in front of us. The bus would stop and one of the candidates would go drive the truck for his test, and the bus would follow. Eventually, the bus stopped and a low voice bellowed my name. I dragged myself through the cold rain to reach the truck. I opened the door to the cab and climbed up high steps to the driver's seat, which was too big to sit in comfortably. I was greeted with the cold, unfriendly eyes of the test proctor, an Army colonel who sat in the passenger seat. With a look of shock, he measured me up and down, his gaze seeming to question how I dared to be there. It was clear that he thought my presence was a mistake. I spoke first in an attempt to break the ice.

"Lieutenant Ponici Rodica, reporting to the road test," I said.

He stared at me in silence for a moment before his annoyance burst forth in a shout, *"Why are you here? Your place is in the kitchen with the pots and pans!"*

I was stunned by his vitriol. I'd expected admiration for my courage, perhaps encouragement for my daring undertaking. What I got was quite the opposite. I didn't know how to react. After all, he was a colonel and I was barely a lieutenant, fresh out of college. I kept quiet since there was nothing I could say that wouldn't annoy him further. I settled in my seat, checked my mirrors, buckled my seatbelt, and hoped for the best, all with the sneaking feeling that I had already failed the driving test, before I'd even started. I waited for his signal to go ahead and take the road test. In the end, he didn't have much choice but to let me drive. He nodded to go ahead, so I did. I drove through the rain, holding back the sense of disappointment and fighting to make it beyond every inch of road.

The test was torture. Not because I couldn't handle the big truck, but because of what I was up against. It was torture because even though I was doing well, I was going to fail. *My place is in the kitchen. Who does he think he is?* Adi had never said such a thing to me and always encouraged me to stand up for myself. Adi's goal was always to build up my strength so that I had a voice in a world that, most of the time, held the same views as that impertinent colonel.

The colonel's voice echoed the earlier thunder of the skies when he finally spoke again to tell me to pull over and stop the truck. My exam was over, as was my agony. I pulled the truck to the side of the road and sat silently waiting for my verdict. I was guilty of having the audacity to step into the world of men. I couldn't stop thinking of how Adi seemed perfectly fine, even proud of, the fact that I broke boundaries.

The waiting was excruciating until the colonel finally handed me a slip of paper and murmured that I passed. He said nothing more, no commentary about sending me back to the kitchen. Was it possible that I'd impressed him?

I forgot about the colonel as soon as I exited the truck. I passed!

I knew Adi would be proud of me. When I told him I passed, he simply said, "I knew you would. You did amazing in practice. You know what you are doing." His confidence in me was unshakable. In the world of men, I'd found a guy who knew that I could be his equal, and who was man enough to take pride in my accomplishments.

16

A JOURNEY OF A THOUSAND MILES BEGINS WITH A SINGLE STEP

Everything happened so fast. Life, as we were living it, came to a sudden and surprising halt. A new chapter was to start, one for which I was not prepared. Not only were there changes and challenges ahead, but we had to drag our little boy along with us on this journey into uncharted territory.

At the time, we'd barely made it out of college, and settled down into an apartment we were proud of. Adi had realized his dream of flying the newest fighter jet, the MiG-29. Riky was just a few weeks shy of his first birthday, and we were happy as a family. By Romanian standards of the time, we were making good money, Adi graduating with a 4,050 lei salary and I with 3,850 lei (compared with my dad who made barely 1,700 lei before he passed away). On my own I was earning what both my parents earned after working almost a lifetime. We had all the hallmarks of dreams fulfilled and a happy life ahead.

The trajectory of our lives started to take a new path one night when I woke with the sudden realization that Adi wasn't next to me. He often came to bed later than I did, so it wasn't uncommon to wake without him there, but at that moment I was keenly aware of unease building inside me. I rubbed my eyes and dragged myself to the living room to make sure he was okay, to convince myself that my feeling of unease was unnecessary. Adi sat on the couch watching television, but his face showed only distress. What he was watching on television was hurting him.

Instinctively, I knew he wasn't ready to talk about it, that he was better left alone for the time being. I retreated to the bedroom.

The next morning, Adi told me he'd been watching a private broadcast of student protesters being beaten in Bucharest. Their protests were in the hopes for a better life. Adi was disappointed by how the "new" Romanian government reacted.

As I replay the conversation in my mind, I realize that it was the moment Adi made up his mind that we should leave Romania. That the time had come to give up on the dream of a better Romanian life. Nothing was getting better, nor was there any hope of improvement in the near future.

While the government suppression and the hardships of the people were normal in Communist times, I found the events that were happening in my country after December 1989 disturbing. I believed that after the revolution of 1989, things would change in some regard, at least when it came to blatant atrocities and abuse of power. Still, I was a patriot who never dreamed of leaving the land where she was born, while something deep inside Adi longed to find a better life elsewhere. He questioned everything, taking nothing at face value. He'd tried to do his part to improve the social and political climate by voicing his beliefs and participating in Bucharest events organized by CADA, a pro-democracy military committee. CADA was formed after the December events and included military personnel from units across the country. They demanded the removal of senior officials, including the defense minister, who'd participated in the pre-Revolution oppression of Romanian people. CADA called for this among other revisions to the military which should have happened but didn't. Despite their efforts, the burden of an unchanged society and lack of progress after the revolution was still too much to bear, so much so that it outweighed Adi's dream of flying in the Air Force. It didn't matter anymore, overshadowed by the lack of social well-being, by the fact that the future didn't look bright for our child. He knew it would have been a continuous struggle to make it in a corrupt and uncertain society. It would take generations to shake off all of the Communist influence.

It wasn't as if he hadn't tried to make it work. Adi was bright. Shortly after the revolution, in early 1990, he had the vision of flying privately. He wanted to open a private airport on the Black Sea seaside. He found the land and arranged to purchase it. Next he went to the airplane factory in Brasov and arranged to have a private plane built. When it came to the air space in Bucharest, he hit his first stumbling block. He was told that there was no such thing as flying privately. The government owned the sky. Only the Air Force and commercial planes were allowed to fly. Adi knew that those policies would change one day, but how long would it take for that to happen? Could his dreams, our lives, and the life of our son be put on hold for an idea as abstract as "someday"? He knew the answer.

While I was growing up, the focus was always on hardships and the immediate needs of my family. Adi had a different background. His family had money and was therefore free from many of the worries that preoccupied my family's world. Adi had a free spirit and grew up questioning everything. He was exposed to information and knew how to judge it. He'd always had a desire to leave the country and its Communism, long before he met me. But when Adi met me he saw that I was content and so, in a way, he got stuck. I didn't recognize his desire to leave, though perhaps I should have. It was right there in front of me, it was in his free spirit, his judgement of society, his nonconformist attitude and the outspokenness that often landed him in trouble. In me, Adi saw patriotism, and he feared that if he divulged his desire to leave, he could lose me. I was happy, but living in the moment and trying to make the best of our situation. Adi was living in the future and seeing our potential, but feeling trapped by a society that would limit that potential.

What Adi saw on television on that fateful night was the June 1990 Mineriad, an orchestrated suppression of anti-government protesters. Demonstrators took to the streets of Bucharest to protest President Iliescu as well as former high-profile Communist Party members who'd been given weighty political positions even after Communism. The president labeled these protestors as a reactionary, extremist element, calling them hooligans and claiming that they were threatening democracy on the streets of Bucharest. He took this one step further by calling on miners and factory workers to fight the "hooligans" and defend their country.

The violence committed by the miners was inconceivable, leading to injuries and deaths among the demonstrators, most of whom were students. Our society's struggle post-Communism was reflected in these events, including the clashing of groups at University Plaza and the Mineriad. When the dust settled, President Iliescu thanked the miners for being a strong and reliable force—in essence he thanked them for the atrocities they committed against peaceful protestors. Needless to say, this news was troubling and shockingly reminiscent of the events that had taken place before December of 1989, before the revolution that was to have ended such injustice. This was at the root of Adi's sleepless night and the others that followed.

After the irrevocable changes in our lives, the press wrote about Romanian pilots emigrating en masse to the US due to poor pay and flight limitations. While that was undoubtedly true, this was not the core motivation for Adi wanting us to leave. It was his disappointment with the events that followed the Romanian Revolution—the revolution that led to the collapse of Communism and Romania and which ended the lives of Elena and Nicolae Ceaușescu—and a corresponding loss of faith in the goal of bringing democracy to Romania. It was finding the freedom to speak his mind without fear of repercussions. Our country wasn't heading in that direction, and conditions deteriorated, slipping incrementally further away from what we'd held dear as our hope for the future. The night of that television broadcast, something in Adi shifted. He knew that our love was strong enough, that I was strong enough, to leave the land I was attached to. The sacrifices we would have to endure would be worth it. When Adi saw those students being beaten on the television, their pain transported itself into our living room and imprinted on my husband's mind and body. It became too much to withstand, along with the reality that it might one day be our child who was beaten while fighting for a better country, our child who could be persecuted for his beliefs. In that moment Adi committed to building a better life for us and for our children.

For our generation, life in the United States represented an unattainable dream. One might just as soon discover and conquer an unknown planet than relocate to the US. There was no more desirable destination than America. The impossibility of ever getting there only intensified its allure.

Though Adi believed the US held potential for a better life, he didn't idealize it to the point of seeing it as unattainable. When a colleague who was desperate to leave the country reached out to Adi for advice, he immediately suggested applying for a US visa. Once the colleague was successful in his visa application, the seed was firmly planted in Adi's mind that we could follow the same path to freedom.

It was less than three years from that fateful television broadcast to when Adi obtained his visa, but once the visa was in hand, the inevitable next steps happened fast. We had no money for his airline ticket, so we resorted to selling our apartment. It sold for $3,500, which was a lot of money for us. The buyer paid half up front and we arranged for me to rent back the apartment for as long as I needed it—for as long as Adi and I would be apart.

In my innocence of that age, part of me believed that Adi would travel to America for a time and then return to us, somehow bringing a better life back home with him. I didn't fully grasp the concept that the three of us would eventually emigrate. As circumstances changed from one day to the next, it was often all I could do to meet our immediate needs, much less ruminate on what the future held.

The reality of Adi leaving grew closer every day. Though I understood that we were moving toward something better, something greater than life as we knew it, it felt like the unravelling of our dreams, our life dissolving into a nightmare.

Despite the stress, I didn't call Nelu to let him know what was happening. The omission wasn't intentional, we'd simply grown apart ever since graduation. When we were still in school, Adi and I knew that the only way for us to be together was in Constanta. We'd talked to Nelu about joining us there. The three of us had strong bonds with one another and wanted to see each other more. Our time together was rare, as Nelu was busy at the Academy in Bucharest while Adi and I were at the Air Force College. Leading up to graduation, we talked more and more about Nelu joining us in Constanta. At the time, he joyfully agreed. "Of course we'll be together," he said with a smile, "We'll always be together." But before I knew it, everything changed. On a visit home, Nelu, my mother and I were talking in the kitchen. The subject of our future assignments came up and my mother said something about Nelu being stationed close to home, at Oradea. This caught me by surprise.

"But Nelu's coming close to Constanta," I said, "to be closer to me and Adi."

My mother whipped her head around from the kitchen table and looked me straight in the eye. "So that's what you think? He's not going to be near you in Constanta! He's going to be close to *me*, in Oradea."

My eyes darted over to Nelu, but he simply stood there, quiet. I felt betrayed. Why hadn't he told me that he'd changed his mind?

Why did she need to have him close to her when she already had her other two sons, as well as plenty of other relatives and friends? I was about to protest when Adi walked into the kitchen. The look on his face told me not to say anything. He took my hand and led me out to the backyard, where tears began to fall down my cheeks. I was devastated.

"I know it hurts," Adi consoled. "I know it would have been amazing for Nelu and Sorina to come to Constanta so we could all be together, but we can't change it. Let them be together. We'll manage." He held me tight.

At the time I thought that Nelu had wanted to be close to Mom, that he had chosen her over me. Later I'd come to realize that he changed his mind only at my mother's persistence. He was a people pleaser, and he was her favorite child. She did everything she could to make sure he stayed close to her. So for the next four years, Adi and I were fairly on our own. It was just the two of us until Riky came along, and then it was just the three of us. Riky was our sunshine, our hope. As he started to walk and talk, our hearts were buoyed with happiness, but tempered by sadness and the realization that we were raising him in a society which wasn't getting better, it was only getting worse.

Adi received his visa in February, the same month during which we celebrated Riky's first birthday. We then bought his airline ticket through a travel agency, so now he had a departure date: March 22, not even a month after getting the visa. After that date, I'd be left on my own to care for our son in a town far away from our families. In one month we sold our apartment, purchased Adi's ticket, gave his dismissal to the Air Force, packed, and made arrangements for me in his absence. On a Sunday morning he left for Bucharest, all of his life packed into a single suitcase and $500 in his pocket. Even today I marvel at the strength it took for Adi to leave the two of us behind. We were his soul and everything he lived for. But his freedom, our freedom, and our collective wellbeing were too important. He was determined to make it right, no matter what sacrifices that might entail. He didn't care what job he'd have to take, a job was just a job. I trusted him. Though I didn't know what the future might hold for the three of us, I knew that I'd follow him to the ends of the earth. I once told him that if he could have taken us to a remote island to live with next to nothing, we would still have been happy if we were all together. He smiled at that thought and said, "Yes, what else would we need?"

After Adi left for Bucharest, I wanted to talk to him once more before he left Romania. Our telephone wasn't working, but I knew that I could drive to our best friends' house to call Adi. My father-in-law had been staying with us to say goodbye to Adi, and I asked him if he would drive me. He said he didn't have a driver's license. Of course, I had my driver's license, but Adi had always done the driving and in all the commotion of preparing for Adi's departure, I hadn't had a chance to practice on our little car that sat out in front of our apartment. I'd mentioned it once, but Adi had said, "You'll be just fine. Just drive it when you need to." I'd never anticipated needing to drive it so soon after he left.

My father-in-law came with me for the drive to my friend's home as a show of moral support. We got in the stick shift and I drove for about a mile before stopping.

"Something's not right," I explained as I pulled to the side of the road. "I think something's wrong with the engine." I just sat there thinking about what I could possibly be doing wrong, when suddenly it clicked. "Dad!" I exclaimed to my father-in-law, "I know what's wrong! Instead of first gear, I took it directly into third gear!" I began driving again and this time the engine worked just fine, despite the fact that I'd periodically stall at a red light and fumble to restart the car while drivers behind me honked in frustration. My father-in-law later told me how scared he'd been as my passenger, but that he had faith in me nonetheless. After a few weeks, the car and I became best friends. We got along fine and I began driving to work as well. Adi was right, as always.

When I managed to reach the phone and dial the number of Nelu's mother-in-law Mamaia, where Adi was staying overnight before his flight the following day, my heart thundered in my chest. I wanted to capture his sweet voice once more before he left the country and make it stay with me forever. Adi's spirits were high and hopeful, while I was a maelstrom of emotion as we talked on the phone. He told me not to worry, to keep my own spirits high as well, and to take care of our little boy.

Adi's heart must have been broken in a million pieces that Sunday when the train pulled away from the station, with me standing on the platform waving goodbye. The present was changing; the future was uncertain. The world that Adi had worked to build around me, to protect me, had just shattered into a million pieces too. I felt alone, left to confront the challenges ahead of me in Adi's absence. Though he knew I was strong and up to the challenge, I still doubted myself. I didn't give voice to my worries though; Adi had enough challenges and worries ahead of him as he was embarking into the unknown, without me reminding him of my own apprehensions. That was us: always worried about the other. And now I was left to care not only for myself, but also our precious little one. It was a big responsibility but one which I embraced, because there was no end to the amount of love and trust we had in each other.

17

HOPE FOR THE BEST, PREPARE FOR THE WORST

After Adi left that Sunday, things would only get harder. The next day I was called into the office at work and informed that I was being grounded. When I asked why, I was told that it was because my husband had left the country for the US; because of that, I would not be allowed to fly for fear that I might try to leave. I attempted to defend myself, told them that Adi would be coming back, but it made no difference. I was grounded, no further explanations given, and that was all there was to it.

The nightmare of Adi leaving us behind, alone and far from family, was big enough to deal with without also having to worry about my job. My work was so much more than a regular job to me, it was a passion. I was a good pilot and a good officer, but now I was grounded because of the government's fear, despite the fact that Communism had fallen three years prior. In the military, nothing had changed.

My life over the next four months became a nightmare. I was quickly identified as the black sheep of the regiment. One by one my previous acquaintances and colleagues began drifting away, until no one else would sit to eat with me in the cafeteria, much less talk to me.

There was another couple, pilots like us, who'd become our best friends. But during this time they were pulled aside and interrogated about our whereabouts and intentions. They were told to stay away and not be associated with us, if they didn't want trouble themselves. Before this time, we'd been inseparable, spending almost every weekend together. We'd visit town or have dinner together, followed by playing cards. I valued our friendship and was devastated to see it needlessly severed even though in our hearts, we still felt close.

Before Adi left, we'd also become friendly with another couple who lived nearby. The wife was a teacher and the husband was a sergeant in our aviation unit. They had a son a few months older than Riky and we enjoyed getting together. After Adi's departure, however, the visits came to a halt. One day I mustered the courage to ask him why they would no longer call or visit. The sergeant told me they were worried.

"Why?" I asked.

"They called my wife," he informed me, "and said that I was having an affair with you."

"But we all know that's not true!" I said in disbelief.

"Yes," he agreed. "And my wife knows that too. But if they are capable of this, what else might they do?"

I understood. Everyone was simply trying to protect their own family. Government surveillance hadn't ended with the fall of Communism, and unscrupulous tactics by counterintelligence units continued. The world in which I lived became less appealing as time went on. Before Adi left, I'd never dreamed of escaping this society, but the cruel reality of life was revealing itself day by day. I'd known that one day I would leave to follow my husband, but I hadn't expected my life to crumble so soon.

Not long after, I was called into the office of the commander, Colonel Tarina. One of the top aviation generals was visiting our unit and wanted to see me. I didn't know what to expect or what I might possibly say. It was a cavernous office flanked on one side by a large desk. I didn't think I'd ever been in that office before, nor did I feel I had any reason to be there on this particular day. It wasn't a good sign. There I was, a second lieutenant, barely twenty-six years of age, being called into an office full of high-ranking, gray-haired officers. The only friendly face I found there was Major Constantinescu, but even his expression was tinged with worry. He'd been kind to me during my hardships of the previous years, but given the circumstances, his high visibility, and escalating tensions, he was no doubt bound in how much he could help me.

When I entered the room, I stepped up to the desk and saluted. The major stepped aside while the commander and general questioned me. The general began outlining my situation, how the powers that be in the military didn't want to make my life miserable, in fact they wanted me to fly again, but they couldn't as long as my husband was away in the US. The only way in which I could think to answer was to declare that Adi would be coming back. The general then posed one of the most unsettling questions I'd ever been asked.

"What if your husband joined the US Air Force? What if he came to fight against us? Would you go back up in the helicopter to fight against him and do your duty?"

Was this really the reason I'd been prohibited from doing my job? I was sure I'd heard it all, but then he continued: "If you divorce your husband, then we will give you your life back."

Despite the gray hair and the high-ranking officers before me, I felt a courage well up inside of me. "I will *not* divorce my husband," I insisted. "If something happens to me, he'll be the one to take care of me. Not you." I felt sharp stares burrowing into me, but I was young and in love. Breaking my family apart was not an option, not even with the distance between Adi and me, not even with the threat of losing more than I already had, losing everything. The men kept speaking but I couldn't hear them. My emotions were too worked up in a frenzy of fighting for my family. Eventually, they dismissed me to return to my duties. I didn't hear anything further from the general after that, which I took to be a good sign.

Adi called me whenever he could, though the calls didn't always go through. On one occasion as we were talking, I overheard distant voices. Was it paranoia or were military personnel listening to our conversations? I was afraid, unsure of what to do or whom to ask for help. The only person I could truly trust was far away and I had my suspicions that our conversations were under surveillance.

One day I went to the public phones at the post office to try to call Adi. I was desperately looking for advice—taking care of our son in the given circumstances was growing unbearable. I felt I was on the losing side of psychological warfare. Relief washed over me when Adi picked up. He understood my desperation and that something needed to change quickly. I was at my limit, on the verge of giving up the Air Force altogether. I contemplated quitting and going to live with Adi's father. Like always, Adi exercised restraint. He didn't tell me what to do. He simply asked me questions, but always let me judge and make my own decisions. During this particular conversation, he did pose a question, presenting a scenario I hadn't considered.

"What if you try to get a US visa and come here? We could leave Riky with my father."

I was stunned by the possibility, shocked as if a bomb had just exploded in close proximity. All I could do was mutter, "Probably."

I left the post office that day wondering what would be best for our family. Not what was best for me or best for Riky or best for Adi, but what was truly best for our family as a whole in the long term. Like every mother, I wanted to be with my child, no matter what. When Adi left, I knew that as long as I could be there for Riky and provide for the two of us, we'd be fine. The hardships at work, however, proved to be unbearable. I needed an escape to keep sane and focus on building a new life for the three of us somewhere else, a new life in America, even if that meant that I might need to leave Romania on my own, before our son could join us.

That night I tossed and turned, unable to sleep, thinking about the options and what it would mean if I left. *Two is always stronger than one*, I thought. I could learn to speak English and get integrated into society sooner. Two minds can judge better, can help and support each other. We'd be able to build our lives faster and better for when Riky would join us.

Riky was just starting to walk at a year old. It was a delight to see him grow; his innocent face and heart helped keep me strong through all of the hardships I was experiencing. When I returned from work each day, I couldn't wait to hug him and hold him tight. He gave me hope for better days when I felt life was crumbling away in a million pieces. Nothing felt natural about the idea of leaving my child and departing for an unknown period of time. Adi had left, but he'd done so with the knowledge that I was there with our child to love and protect him for the both of us.

For a moment I thought about calling Nelu, but we weren't speaking much those days; I did not consider consulting any other of my family members. Later, Nelu would tell me how hurt he was by the fact that I didn't reach out to him during such a difficult time. He would have been there for me.

By morning I was a mess: tired, scared, and confused about my next steps. I readied myself for work and when the babysitter arrived, I left with a breaking heart. I took my car to work, not only because it was fuel efficient and I could afford it, but also because I'd been commuting by car more and more. I could no longer bear boarding the military bus and watching people shift nervously in my presence, taking care to avoid eye contact. I'd been marginalized and no one dared to speak up on my behalf.

As I drove I considered all the ways that my life had been made miserable, despite the fact that I was a good pilot and officer and had never given anyone cause to believe otherwise. I made my decision: if it was possible, I would leave and help Adi make a life for ourselves in the US so that we could reunite our family and get Riky with us as soon as possible. I knew there was no chance of getting a visa for me and Riky both. But how was I to leave town and get a visa when I'd been told not to even leave the city of Constanta? Colonel Tarina would never grant me permission.

Within the next few days I made another trip to the post office to call Adi from a public phone. I told him of my dilemma and he suggested calling the wife of the second in command of Romanian Aviation, Major General Mircea Budiaci. We had met the pair at an air show in Bucharest a few years before and had quickly connected. They'd invited us to their house once, which was a privilege. They'd come across as kind people, willing to help.

"She could invite you over to visit her in Bucharest," Adi suggested. "And while you're there you can run and get the visa."

I knew right away that this was not only a decent plan, but also likely my only chance. I called her and after a little chitchat asked her if she could call my aviation unit, talk to the commander, and ask permission on my behalf so that I could come and see her.

"Because I'd really like to come and see you," I added, my hopes high.

"I'd like that," she responded, "but I really don't carry much weight anymore because I'm divorcing my husband."

"Does anyone know about the divorce yet?" I asked. "Is it public?"

"No, it isn't," she admitted.

"Then no one would suspect a thing," I pleaded. "Please call."

"I will," she answered, agreeing to attempt the call around 10:00 a.m. the following morning.

All I could think about the next day was what result the conversation would yield. Shortly before 10:00 a.m. I went to the Central Phone Room. Soldiers on duty were redirecting external conversations. As a second lieutenant, I figured I had a good chance of them listening to me because I outranked them. When I politely asked to listen to the phone conversation when Mrs. Budiaci called Commander Colonel Tarina, they couldn't see any harm in it. I told them the truth, that she'd be calling to request permission for me to visit her. A soldier handed me a headset to listen in when the call came through.

"Hello," I heard the commander say. "How are you dear Mrs. Budiaci?"

I could hardly believe what I was hearing. His voice sounded like honey, so sweet. I'd never imagined he was capable of sounding like that. They chatted for a bit before she bluntly asked, "Can Second Lieutenant Ponici visit me in Bucharest? I would like to see her."

There was a pause, a hesitation, likely as the commander weighed the consequences of denying her request. Then, he acquiesced, in that sweet voice which had always been so harsh when speaking to me. It still rings in my ears, even today. How ironic, I thought, the difference in his voice when speaking to me, versus when talking to the wife of someone more important. Regardless, I was thankful for his answer. I was going to Bucharest.

I quickly got in touch with the tourist agency we'd used when arranging for Adi's travel. Luckily, I already had my passport. With foresight I now fully appreciated, Adi had insisted we procure passports right after the fall of Communism. Prior to that, we'd been prohibited from having passports; they were issued only for special cases, and even then the travelers had to hand their passports in at the police station at the conclusion of their trip.

On a chilly May morning, I embarked on a train to Bucharest at 4:00 a.m., the earliest train there was. Even though I had permission to leave the city of Constanta, I was afraid of being followed. Before 7:00 a.m. I was already in line at the US embassy in Bucharest to wait for an interview. At that time there were no appointments or computers, you simply had to get in line and wait your turn.

When I was finally called to the window to hand in my papers, I was greeted by a woman with a friendly smile. She took my papers, told me to wait a moment, then walked to a back room where I overheard her speaking to her colleagues. "You won't believe it! We have a woman helicopter pilot today!" Her excitement was a boost to my spirits. It raised my confidence that it would end well. When I later heard my name called, I approached the window thinking that my entire life depended on this moment. Our dreams could be dashed or upheld in the next few minutes. My feelings were an accumulation of years of hopes and sorrow for a better life, and now they could be either put at ease or buried forever. Embracing myself with the confidence that Adi was trusting in me, I answered all of their questions. At the end of the interview, the woman told me to return to pick up my passport, along with the visa, later that afternoon. Those simple words could not have meant more to me and my family. Afraid to show my excitement, I thanked her and left the embassy with the light steps of knowing we had hope for a bright future.

Leaving the US embassy, I rushed to take the bus to the Budiacis' house. I arrived before noon and spent the afternoon with her. She'd opened a small business and her days were busy. She seemed to love what she was doing and wasn't bothered much by her impending divorce. She had a strong personality and I knew, instinctively, that she would be okay.

I purchased the airline ticket through the travel agency, paying over US$800 in total. Later I would learn that the ticket itself was hardly US$500. The extra US$300 that the agency charged was a lot of money in those times. Communist habits die hard, and in essence they took advantage of my ignorance, having no idea that I could have purchased the ticket myself.

My time in the military unit grew more harsh with each passing day. It grew to a boiling point where I felt I could no longer handle the pressure. I told Adi that I was going to get my dismissal earlier than planned, then I'd go live with his father in the interim before my departure to the US. We both agreed that this was a better and safer course of action than remaining in my current circumstances.

The next day when I was in the aviation unit, I went to my commander and informed him that I wished to be dismissed from the Air Force. He handed me a form to fill out, which included a section in which I was supposed to list my reason for requesting a dismissal. I wrote the truth. I held nothing back and detailed how the military had made my life miserable. I knew that it wouldn't make any difference, but I felt a sense of validation by putting the truth down on paper. By that point, I was no longer afraid. I handed in the paper.

Days passed and nothing happened. Every day I reported for duty and waited for a resolution. I couldn't understand what was going on. Then one day I commuted to work by military bus. We were ready to head home in the evening; everyone had boarded the bus and we waited for it to leave. For some reason, the bus wasn't moving. Then a man boarded the bus, called out my name, and asked me to go with him. He took me to the commander's office. I felt as if I was walking to my own execution. I had no idea what to expect and worry took hold of me.

The commander sat behind his desk with my dismissal form in hand. "I can't send this in," he said. "At least not the way it was written. Moreover, it's been over two weeks since you turned this in and the new law requires us to hand in all dismissal paperwork within two weeks of it being written."

Now I understood. They were in trouble. They felt that I should be in trouble for what I'd written, but at the same time they were in trouble for holding onto my dismissal letter too long and failing to turn it in.

"I'll tell you what we'll do," the commander continued. "You write what we tell you in a new dismissal form with today's date, and we'll make sure it gets handed in and approved as soon as possible. You'll get your wish."

It felt like blackmail, but I had little choice. My main objective was to get out unharmed and as soon as I could. I reluctantly rewrote the dismissal paper and handed it in. With mixed feelings I returned to the bus, which had been held up to wait for me. When I boarded, I felt the eyes of my colleagues on me, wondering what had happened. I quietly took my seat, ready to cry but refusing to do so. My pain was mine to bear, as it had proven to be, time and time again. No one reached out or stood by me; they couldn't even if they'd wanted to. They became strangers to me, while I became a stranger to my aviation family of almost four years. I was alone on that bus full of people, but at least I was on my way to being free. Truly free.

18

NATURE WILL HAVE ITS COURSE

When I want to think about childhood, I picture my grandmother's house in the country. Although I lived there for only three years, it seems to me that I have lived there since the day I was born. Because it held such value for me, after an absence of many years I went to say goodbye to that place and to the people I loved before departing for the US.

As I approached Burda county, I was flooded with memories of old times. I felt like a child again. The world appeared smaller than it was. My car drove through Burda, apparently knowing the destination, and the dust of the county roads was disturbed, together with my soul.

Here was my grandmother's house. I expected it to be bigger than it was. As rain fell and winds blew, the color of the house was lost. I do not remember if it was a sunny day or cloudy day, but it seemed time had dulled this place I'd once called home, casting a gray hue upon the structure. My aunt, daughter to my grandmother, descended the stairs, surprised to see me. She was the same strong person I'd remembered her to be, with brown eyes which could go through my body and touch my heart with kindness.

"Your uncle is not home, he went to see the land," she said.

"I want to see him and I do not have much time," I said. "Let's go find him."

We left the car there. It seemed unreal in that quiet environment, and my steps took me on the same path as they used to years ago:

to the land.

Here was the river. It ran large, deep, and tumultuous. I remembered my grandmother washing clothes in the river as I played nearby or tried to help her. She was smaller than I am now but she was my childhood. My world was around her. She left me independent but never alone. But after so many years, I felt my own peace uncertain in contrast to the quiet river, and the water was not higher than my knees.

"Look what the river did!" I exclaimed. It dug into my grandmother's land. She knew that it would happen one day. There had been a lot of trees, but only a few of them remained.

I stepped on my grandmother and uncle's land, and then I saw my uncle. In childhood we did a lot of things together. He played with me and I helped him in the garden. I actually thought he was a child too. He was tall, strong, with black hair like crows' feathers and beautiful eyes. He was deaf but we understood each other well. I looked at him now. He was smaller than me. His hair was gray and wrinkles invaded his face. Still, his eyes were the same, carrying love for his land and for me. What a privilege for me to be compared with his land! The land was everything to him. I think his body was made of the land.

When we returned to the house he showed me my old chair and my old bed. *How had I slept in a bed filled with straw?*, I asked myself. My uncle still slept in one. My aunt bought him "modern" furniture, but he did not accept it. He accepted electricity though. Oh, I remembered the gas lamp. One night I played too late and when I got home I realized that I hadn't studied my history lesson.

"The lamp is not good for your eyes," worried my grandmother. "Go to bed. You can study tomorrow." That night was as long as my history class the following day.

The stove was the same one as in my childhood. My grandmother used to bake such delicious cookies! That house was full of her and everything had her fingerprints on it. Her soul was imprinted into the very core of the building. I turned to my uncle and with a soft voice told him, "I want to go to my grandmother's grave." Life had been severe to me; I'd not been able to go to her funeral and now I wanted amends.

My uncle took my hand and said, "Let's go."

We arrived at the place where my grandmother's body had been laid to rest. That cemetery where, at one time, I'd been visiting my grandfather's grave with my grandmother, was for me in childhood a place to run around, but now a painful place with real graves. Though her grave was full of flowers, it was glacial and repulsive. I thought with sadness of my grandmother's final months. She died five months after my father, perhaps of a broken heart. She found out about his death only after the funeral had taken place, and so carried with her the despair of a mother who hadn't known when her child was ill and dying, and also had missed the opportunity to be at his funeral.

Standing at her grave, suddenly I could feel my grandmother's presence as sure as I could feel myself living. I could hear her voice as I could hear the birds singing above us. Everything was a mystery, but at the same time I made peace with myself. I knew that even if my grandmother was in the unknown universe, she still loved me. And it was my turn to love and to take care of my little boy. This is life's irony: as time passes, some lives appear and some disappear.

The wind blew the leaves around the grave as a sign that my meeting with my grandmother was over. I left the cemetery knowing that a part of my heart remained and belonged there. She had been my friend, my sister, and my mother. She combed my hair, prepared breakfast, and waited for me when I came home from school. She was like a soldier in her actions, never missing a call to duty, to sacrifice herself for others.

I left my grandmother's county and my uncle with sadness. Although I knew that nothing would be the same, I still hoped that, maybe, something would take the same shape as before. What would be that "something"? A house, a tree, a river, or a memory? I've since heard that my aunt wants to sell my grandmother's house and the land. It is inevitable that my next meeting with the past will be more painful. Perhaps there will not be a next meeting. I have lost the house, the tree, the river. I want, at least, to keep my memories intact.

19

TWO SHORTEN THE ROAD

Leaving us behind was unbearable, and without question the most difficult thing Adi had ever done. He left not knowing for how long we'd be separated. He didn't know how long we'd be apart, only that he would be unable to care for us, to protect us, during that time. He must have felt powerless the same way I felt one morning when I left my sleeping son to begin my journey to be reunited with Adi.

We'd always said that two was better than one. We knew that we were stronger together, but the sacrifices that had to be made were too big to carry, too crushing to endure.

Leaving Riky was the first time I felt my heart physically hurt. I heard it shattering into tiny pieces and it took my breath away. My body moved, my lips formed words, but immense pain wreaked havoc through my body, starting from my heart, impairing my mind, running through me from head to toe. Hurling pain all over, then starting again from the beginning. Every time I thought it couldn't get worse, I learned I'd been mistaken.

I couldn't stop crying, uncontrollable crying. I didn't know what I was doing or what the future held. Though I knew we were doing what was best given the circumstances, I just didn't care about the circumstances anymore. I wanted my child. I wanted to hug him and care for him. I wanted to see his sweet smile and feel his little hands hugging me back. Was that too much to ask?

That little boy was more than our sunshine, he was our universe. And while I knew that our decision for me to leave was best for him in the long run, a mother's emotions aren't built to withstand parting from her own child. It was the greatest sacrifice of my life and the most difficult one I'd ever have to make. Nothing else could compare, not leaving my country, my town, the Air Force, my mother or brothers, none of it came close to leaving my sleeping son one morning. No mother should have to choose between freedom and her child.

As I readied myself that morning to go to the train station, I tried not to make too much noise. Riky slept peacefully on that warm July morning, and I was all too aware that I wouldn't be coming home that night to tuck him back into bed. I watched his sweet face and restrained myself from hugging him. I didn't want to wake him.

Refusing to think and give in to the unbearable feelings, I headed out before dawn into the darkness of night. Had I been traveling by foot to Bucharest instead of by train, I would have walked backwards to see his sweet smile one more time, but the train kept taking me forward. I wondered when I would see my son again, but couldn't let my mind follow through with that thought entirely. It hurt too much. It didn't make sense to give up my son for a dream so uncertain and undefined.

Will I ever see my son again? I asked myself. *Am I doing the right thing?* And what even was the right thing to begin with? When my husband had asked me to get the visa, it was not a request or demand, it was my decision whether or not to go through with it. If I wanted to. But how could I not want to? It would be far easier to build our new life with the two of us working together than if we continued to exist a world apart. We were building a future for our family. The sacrifices were all for the little boy left behind. Adi had the audacity and fearlessness to take those initial steps, and I wanted to be reunited with him to help him—to help us. Not only would it be easier with the two of us side by side, but I felt it would also be faster, and the three of us would be reunited as a family sooner. The sacrifices would be worth it in the end. That mindset was how I was able to turn the pain of leaving our son into determination and endurance to apply to our future and strength to move forward. It became a wish to build a new life for him and have him join us as soon as possible. At that moment I could have moved mountains. Instead of focusing on the torture of my soul, I opened up my heart to the high hopes of being reunited with Adi and joining the struggles and aspirations to start a new life in a new world. Though my feelings remained conflicted, I began to look to the future and hope for better days instead of dwelling in my pain.

My heart was an endless fountain of love for both my son and my husband. Despite the pain of leaving Riky, my excitement at the prospect of being reunited with Adi continued to grow. I bought new clothes just for the trip, just for him. I wore a white, pleated skirt that fell just above the knee, a white blouse and white sandals. It was July and I was heading for a new and pure life, and white was the color for it. Maybe the purity of white was balancing out the guilt of leaving our son behind.

The train ride and my time at the airport were uneventful. I was nervous that at any moment, something would happen that would keep me from making it out of the country, but I did. It was the first time I held a passport in my hand for my inaugural voyage on a commercial plane. The flight was wonderful and full of hope. I remember using broken English to try to tell the passenger next to me about being reunited with Adi. How could I hold a conversation with someone when I knew only a handful of words in English? Yet I couldn't sit still and had to try. The eight hours flew by as fast as the plane cutting through the sky. As we neared landing, I marvelled at so many trees below. They represented life, new life, and I felt excitement coursing through my body like the giddiness of a small child. I couldn't wait to get off that plane and see Adi again.

Adi had my flight information and I knew he'd be there waiting for me. What was on his mind? Was he already driving after only a few months in the US? Would he be the same positive force of nature as I'd known him to be? Would he have the same mix of joy and sadness that filled my heart?

After deplaning, I made my way towards customs. My heart beat heavy in my chest. Even though I had a visa, this was the moment when my entrance would be denied or accepted. We'd faced so many trials, it would not have surprised me for this to be yet another. What if they sent me back? But they didn't, and getting that stamp on my passport and being waved through, essentially into America, felt like a pivotal moment in my greater journey.

I retrieved my luggage and frantically began scanning faces in the airport, looking for Adi. I couldn't get my eyes on him fast enough. And there he was, an incandescent smile on his face, waving his arms and coming my way. We embraced, sweet and long like I never wanted to let him go, never again.

Adi helped me with my luggage as we left the airport. The hot summer air washed over me and lifted a weight off my shoulders. The day felt fresh and full of hope. *This is the feel and smell of freedom*, I thought. Once on the sidewalk, Adi told me to wait while he went to bring the car around. I watched as an endless parade of beautiful, gleaming cars drove past, wondering which one Adi was driving. Then a car, little more than a heap of metal and rust, stopped and Adi got out to help me with the luggage. When I went to open the back door, he stopped me.

"The door will fall off. It's not working," he explained. The Chevy Cavalier was beyond ancient, and discolored from time in ways I hadn't thought possible, with rust that created a rainbow of browns. "Someone gave it to me for free as long as I pay the insurance," Adi said proudly. And I was proud of him. He made things happen against the odds, including procuring a vehicle.

The drive from JFK airport to Ridgewood, Queens, was amazing.

We were reunited, together again, it was *us* again. Luckily we didn't need much beyond each other, because our apartment on Seneca Avenue was poorly maintained. Adi had a lone mattress on the floor in what was supposed to be a bedroom. We didn't have pillows and didn't buy any either, because we didn't want to spend the money on them. As a result, we woke every morning to stiff necks. The kitchen, covered in a thick veneer of grease, was home to a small table and two chairs. Cockroaches ran everywhere. Though I cleaned as much as I could, the apartment was in deplorable condition, and cleaning could only do so much. Without air conditioning, we were forced to sleep with the windows open, kept awake at night by the sounds of honking and loud music drifting up from the streets below.

Adi was able to take a few days off from work to stay with me after I first arrived. We'd walk along Seneca Avenue, holding hands and smelling the freedom in the air. Those days were glorious and nothing bothered us, not the apartment or the fact that we didn't have money or good jobs. We didn't care. We had each other and knew that as long as we were together, we would survive and succeed. It was in our power to fight for a better life, to learn English and go back to school. Instead of seeing the hardships which we were up against, we saw the potential of fulfilling our dreams. The smell of freedom was indescribable and feeling freedom for the first time was priceless.

When I left Romania, I had no idea what my identity and my family's identity would become. I was only dreaming of a better life. One of my identity changes came, unintentionally, in the spelling of my first name, from Rodica to Rodika. The difference came down to the sound of the letter "c" versus "k." Since I was a little girl, I'd placed great emphasis on my name being pronounced correctly, and even in adulthood, this was more important than the spelling of it. If changing my first name gave me a better chance at correct pronunciation, so be it.

Name change aside, we loved every minute of those first few months that we lived in the dilapidated apartment in Ridgewood. After taking a few days off for my arrival, Adi had to return to work because we were running out of money. He worked on the roof of a building next to Central Park in Manhattan, pouring tar on hot summer days, often in temperatures over 100 degrees Fahrenheit.

For a few days I accompanied Adi to work, waiting on a bench in Central Park, admiring everything around me and basking in the possibilities. I was happy and content. Though a part of us was missing, the future looked bright. The subway's graffiti and miserable stations did nothing to dampen the joy I felt at my newfound homeland. Beauty surrounded us, and I knew it was worth suffering and fighting to make it happen.

We never took pity on ourselves; what we went through was simply our new, normal life, what we endured emotionally, financially, and socially were the building blocks of our future. We took every day as it came. We didn't have much money, so everything we received was more than welcome. I got a light brown, polyester coat to keep warm in the winter, though it wasn't heavy enough for the New York cold and the wind blew through it. For five dollars I bought a black pair of shoes, but before long my big toe poked through and water would seep in between my toes. With two dollars I purchased a hat to keep my head warm. In a thousand ways like these, we were able to make do.

Two months after I arrived in the US we moved to a better apartment on Gates Avenue. We furnished it with furniture either given to us or found on the street, and we proudly called it home. Our apartment, and the building at large, was old and unimproved. While our landlords felt it was fine as it was, Adi and I committed to making improvements when we could. We renovated the bathroom, including replacing the floor by the big bathtub, so that you could no longer see through the floor to the basement. For the bathroom, we were reimbursed for the materials, though our landlords declined to do the same when we replaced the kitchen countertops, arguing that the previous countertops had been perfectly acceptable. They were a kind couple, but I couldn't understand why they viewed the conditions as acceptable. We didn't question it, and luckily we were used to dealing with things on our own.

Along our journey it was difficult to find encouragement, or even good advice when faced with difficult decisions. It was a new society with new rules, and we had to learn the hard way to trust our own judgement. In the beginning I got a job as a babysitter for a six-month-old baby. I didn't know how to speak English, but the family trusted my background and gave me the chance to learn the language, which I did so right along with the baby. A lot of times I saw Riky in the baby and to be able to take care of him was a privilege.

I knew I needed to return to college to succeed in American society, but I struggled to settle on a major. My father had dreamed that I might become a doctor, and I decided on nursing since it required less school. Initially I got my nurse aide certificate to get a feel for the work and earn some money while going back to college. I began volunteering and working in hospitals. The work was both difficult and sporadic, but forty-five dollars per day was too much to pass up.

On one occasion, the nursing agency assigned me to care for a hospital patient for a few days. The patient was a tall, imposing, and tattooed middle-aged man who intimidated me with his physicality, coupled with aggressive and foul language to which I was unaccustomed. He held nothing but disdain for the hospital and its staff that tried to care for him. To calm him, I continually agreed with him, despite his unsavory behavior, such as spitting on all of the paintings lining the hallway as I'd accompany him to lunch. Once seated, he'd curse at anyone in earshot and either spit in his food or push it away. My first day with him shook me terribly, but we needed the money and so I returned to the assignment the following day. In time, he grew calmer in my presence. He began to listen to me, so I quickly seized the opportunity to tell him that his actions landed me in trouble.

"What do I need to do to not get you in trouble?" he asked. "You're nice to me. I want to help you." These words hit my ears like a miracle.

"Well," I ventured, "when we go for lunch it would be nice if you didn't spit on the walls."

He agreed. His behavior continued to improve and I daresay that by the end of my assignment, we got along fine and even enjoyed one another's company.

Despite that particular happy ending, soon enough I knew that nursing wasn't the career for me, as I began "dying with the patients." I was unable to detach myself emotionally and just do my job. I was too passionate about caring for people and ended up suffering along with them, as in the case of one of my patients in her seventies. We chatted every night, until the evening I arrived at my shift to find her bed empty. She'd died of cancer that morning.

After realizing that I wasn't going to continue along the path of nursing, Adi mentioned the possibility of me pursuing a career in information technology. In the mid-nineties IT was booming. I pondered the idea. When we gathered with some friends for a birthday party, I mentioned it and was immediately shot down.

"IT is too difficult. You have to study constantly to keep up with the changes. I wouldn't recommend it," one of our friends said.

On the way home, Adi could tell that I was upset. I told him of the conversation and he said, "I don't know why he said that, but I wouldn't trust that advice, even if he works in the field himself. You can do anything you set your mind to. If you want to work in IT, go for it. You'll be in the top ten percent of them." He spoke with a confidence and calm that soothed me. And I trusted him. He was my voice of reason and I believed him. Incidentally, my trust in Adi's words was well founded; I would eventually manage to do well in my career in IT, though it wasn't easy.

When I was accepted to CUNY, I received a letter advising me to be at the college auditorium at a specified date and time. I had no idea what for and I found myself in an auditorium full of students waiting to take an exam. After the test, I learned that the purpose was to evaluate our reading and writing levels for English. I failed. That summer I went to the admissions office and my advisor said, "Yes, you failed, but you got 30 out of 32 at reading, and 5 out of 8 at writing. You have two teachers for writing and one of them gave you a 3. You'll pass if both give you a 4 and you're very close to passing. Come to summer school. It's free and then most likely you'll pass and be able to start in the fall with the right level of English classes."

I followed his advice, managing work around the early classes. I retook the reading exam and passed, and only had the writing exam left to conquer. As I neared the end of the summer class, I shared my confidence of passing the writing test with friends, but found my confidence shattered once again.

"What makes you think you'll pass?" an acquaintance asked. "Eighty percent of the *American* students don't pass. I don't think you'll pass the test."

Her husband, noting my expression of disappointment, retorted, "If she thinks she can do it, she can do it."

And I did. I passed. That fall I was able to enroll in the college English course.

My English professor was amazing and it was in that course where I discovered my passion for writing, which I realized via a succession of essay assignments. During one class, she returned all of the essays but mine, and I couldn't understand why. Then she looked at me and asked, "Would you mind if I read your essay to the class?"

"No," I replied. "I don't mind." I was wondering why she would want to do so since I could barely speak in English and my writing was poor. It was quiet in class as she read my words with passion in her intonation. In that moment I recognized my passion for crafting with words. One of my essays would go on to win first prize in the college writing contest. The college organized an event in the auditorium where all students and families were invited. Students who won first prizes in writing, poetry, and other literary categories had to present their work. I was petrified to read from my essay in front of so many people, but I tried my best to practice the paragraphs I had selected to read, which were the last ones of the essay. I still remember getting up there on the stage with my essay in my hand and a heavy stone in my heart. Adi was in the audience and his presence helped to give me strength in that moment. When I started reading everyone grew quiet. Too quiet, I thought. I finished reading and there was no reaction from anyone. I thought I'd failed and started heading back to my seat when the audience erupted in thunderous applause. As I passed audience members, I was greeted with words of encouragement that I'd done an amazing job. I knew then that my teacher was right to have believed in me and submitted my work to the contest. I've often joked that, had I been born in the US, I would have been an editor. It would have suited me well, but my career path was leading in a different direction.

Throughout the years many people have asked me to write my story. "You are an inspiration," they say. "People would enjoy having you share your story." It's taken time to focus on it, but it's been a fulfilling and worthwhile endeavor. I'm forever grateful to my English teacher who returned essays with comments urging me to finish my story.

That's not to say my writing was always received well. At Baruch College I took an advanced English class. At the beginning of the semester we were challenged to look at the curriculum and write an essay proving that any topic included in it was inappropriate to teach. If we proved our point, then we would be able to skip the course and receive an "A." This was an opportunity I desperately wanted to take advantage of. I really could have used that "A," and forgoing class would have helped ease my busy schedule.

Riding the subway back home, inspiration suddenly hit me and I began writing right there. When my essay was revised and polished, I handed it in. The course curriculum covered English history up to the 1800s, starting with the Bible. I thought that was inappropriate since there were students in the class from wildly differing backgrounds, and indeed some students got up, left the class, and dropped the course when reading the curriculum. In writing, I stated my case. For a few classes after turning in my essay, the teacher said nothing. I finally approached her about it, but she avoided giving me a clear answer. By the middle of the semester I had an "A-" in her class, and she finally told me that I had a very good essay and successfully proved my point, but that she wasn't allowed to have me skip the course entirely. It was against policy.

"Why did you offer the chance then?" I asked, feeling cheated.

"I never had a student take up the challenge," she said. "You are the first to take it and then manage to prove it, too."

Though I was disappointed that she didn't keep her promise, one that I had taken quite seriously, I continued to study hard and managed to achieve that 'A-' on my own, despite that it was an advanced English class. I think the professor appreciated and honored my effort, because by the end of the semester she'd converted my "A-" to an "A."

Aside from our thoughts of Riky, Adi and I were too busy learning English and working to give too much thought to the world we'd left behind, including my prior life in the Air Force and my former colleagues. That's why I couldn't understand why I had a recurring dream. College had apparently left a huge imprint on me. In the dream I was about to leave Air Force college after graduation. I packed feverishly, worried that I might forget something. It was taking too long and images of things that I cared about flashed before me, as if I was really there. When I finished packing, I left the apartment, descended the stairs, and dragged my suitcase along a mile of road to the train station.

I wondered where the dream came from. Was it that I didn't want to leave? Did it root in my worries about starting a new life away from the college's comfort and protection? Deep down, I knew that the place encompassed a huge part of my life. It was the girls I'd spent so much time with, going through the same emotions, sharing the same aspirations, and chasing the same dreams. We all approached it with different perspectives; nevertheless, we all desperately wanted to be there. It was the apartment building where we struggled to keep warm in the winter, where we'd heat water to bathe and forgo sleep for our studies. It was the planes and hangars and airfield where we spent our summers learning to fly. It was the buildings where we studied, craving more knowledge with each passing day. It was the teachers and talented instructors who inspired us to do our best. It was all of that, and the fact that I was able to do it with Adi by my side.

But it was my second recurring dream that wouldn't leave me alone. We were in our apartment in Constanta. Our first apartment. The events within the dream might vary, but we were always there, it was that first apartment I dreamt about. Was it because it was the first place the three of us had been together as a family? Was it regret that I wanted us to be back there, happy again?

I never returned to Constanta. I've had opportunities to go, but didn't. After many years, I was able to reconnect with the most important person of my career as an officer in the Romanian Air Force, Paul Constantinescu. I was overjoyed to be in contact with him again and always envisioned seeing him on a return trip, to properly thank him for all he'd done for me. When a few months passed with no response from him, I made inquiries only to learn that he'd recently died. And along with him perished my opportunity to give him the thanks that he so deserved. I will forever be grateful for the role he played in my life.

Sorrow gives way to gratitude, not only in regards to the people we've lost, but also the places we've left behind, like Constanta, which played such a pivotal part in my journey. Nonetheless, I never returned, perhaps wanting to burn the past and the pain that came with it. As a result, I forwent all opportunities to visit that place of our first apartment. Leaving meant moving forward into a new life, one in which I envisioned being together with Adi and Riky, for there was nothing in the world I needed more.

20

ALL'S WELL THAT ENDS WELL

Our utmost desire was to be reunited with Riky. We would have done anything to be with him, to be able to touch his sweet face and hold tight to his tiny body. The cumbersome process of gaining permanent US residency was difficult and painful for every immigrant, and my family was no exception. That interminable waiting for an end to the immigration process, a process that was easily swallowed by its own paperwork.

The immigration process was fraught with challenges at every step. Adi applied for an H-1B visa through his employer, but it was taking too long, forever caught in limbo, and we just couldn't wait anymore. We reached our threshold of reasoning with ourselves that one day the three of us would be together. We longed to be reunited and could wait no more. Separation from our son could go no further into the abyss of time.

One possible end to our dilemma was finding another country that would have offered us a home. We filled out an application for residency in New Zealand, applying for work on my skills as a helicopter pilot. Our application was denied, having garnered only twenty-eight points. The prior year, twenty-eight points was the minimum necessary to get approved, but the year we applied, they'd raised the minimum to twenty-nine. We were one point shy of being accepted. Disappointed and heartbroken, we decided to then try for Australia. This time our application rested on the merits of Adi's engineering skills. It was also denied, but came with a promising note: to reapply in a few months when Adi had six months of experience as an engineer. His job was simply too new. They also refunded our application money, a small gesture for them, but one which meant the world to us. We set our sights on reapplying in December of that year, but in October, we had a breakthrough in the US. We gained the right to bring Riky to join us through Adi's employer. Realizing we could bring our son over caused our emotions to run high, but we also still knew that the journey we were embarking on to make it happen would be long and arduous. On October 5, 1995, I journaled my thoughts and joy:

> *We thank you, God, for listening to our prayers.*
> *We thank you, God, for being able to get our son.*
>
> *I can't imagine that in as little as a month from now, I'll be able to hold tight to my child in my arms. It's incredible!*
>
> *Adi just called to let me know that the visa was approved. How I've dreamt about this moment. Our own son becomes a reality for us. Now he will be reunited with us.*
>
> *God, help me have him now and I'll never let go of my child from my side or his father's again.*
>
> *God, help me find the strength to finish college and for all to be well.*
>
> *Now I can write the letters I've always meant to and go through the photographs. I can share my thoughts on paper, thoughts I've been afraid to confront because the pain of separation is too great. I can look at the pictures with hope instead of sadness. I'm no longer afraid of bringing back the memories of having a son, which life has denied me.*

ENOUGH LOVE

It seems as if today, life has taken on a new meaning.

My hope of seeing my son within a month was overly ambitious. It would take another six months before we'd have his passport and visa, and for Riky to land at JFK airport. The passport process should have been very simple, but ended up taking forever, and Adi's dad worked tirelessly through the application in Romania. During that time, even though we had the right to be reunited with our son and the paperwork to prove it, we went through fears that it would never happen. It was difficult to shake the feeling of being scared that our hopes would be irrevocably crushed, as if a hidden foe might suddenly destroy everything we'd been striving for. Logically, nothing could prevent us from being united, but the obstacles we faced at every turn pushed us further into a state of desperation and we couldn't shake the feeling of being hopeless in the face of destiny.

The first three years in the US were difficult. We had to start a new life in a new language and a new society. Learning to adapt was challenging enough, but doing it without our son made it unbearable most of the time. In the beginning, we tried to call every week just to hear his sweet voice, even though the phone calls were terribly expensive. After a while, we began calling every few weeks, but even then we talked more with Adi's father than with Riky, who was too busy growing up and playing as children do. We'd often hear him playing in the background and when my father-in-law would beckon him to the phone to talk with us, Riky would say, "Dad, do I have to talk? Can't I just go play?" It would break our hearts, not because Riky was calling Adi's father "Dad" instead of "Grandpa," because for that we were happy. It was a comfort to know that Riky loved my father-in-law, because in our absence we knew that he was loved. The heartbreak came when we realized that Riky was losing his connection to us, that we were slowly drifting into strangers to him. That hurt too much, and in time, perhaps we began unwittingly to call less frequently to avoid the hurt. Riky didn't know who we were anymore and I worried that we were little more than a bother to him. Adi's dad and Olga did their best to remind Riky of us, but we'd left him at such a young age, when he'd just started to walk and talk. We weren't there for the first time his small steps became an act of running. We missed out on moments that can never be regained, like Riky awkwardly learning to dress himself. We never heard him speak his first sentences or tell us that he loved us while looking into our eyes.

At a garage sale in upstate New York, we found a clown doll. It was in good condition and evoked a feeling of peace with its bright colors and cute hat. We purchased the doll and I dressed it in a vest that I'd knitted for Riky when he was a baby. I had a few of his things with me so that I could run my fingers over them and be reminded of him. Riky's vest fit the doll perfectly. Every night, exhausted after a long day, we'd drag ourselves to the bedroom to welcome a good rest, and I'd take the doll I'd come to think of as "Rikita" in my arms. I'd hold him, hug him, tell him goodnight, and then cry myself to sleep. It was my routine and offered me a small sense of comfort. At the same time, there were nights when holding the doll made me feel a disconnect in my soul, and a powerlessness reflected back on me as I watched the clouds glide across the vast expanse of sky. Being without our child, and holding a doll in his stead, felt comforting and necessary, but also as if I was plunging into an abyss, over and over again.

When I'd see babies or small children with their parents, I couldn't help but think: *Hug them and love them! You are so fortunate to be able to do so.* Those months of waiting were torture. Our hopes and dreams were about to come to life, if only we were able to hold our child in our arms once again.

My journal entry from April 3, 1996, read:

Finally! I am on the subway heading to meet Adi so that we can go to the airport together. Riky is coming! Our dear and loved little boy is coming. I know it will be very difficult for awhile, but now all three of us will be together. Nothing can fill my heart with happiness more than Riky's arrival. Gosh, what emotions I have! And Adi feels just the same. We haven't seen him in almost three years.

Adi and I are exhausted. We almost managed to finish renovating the apartment, mainly the bathroom. I hope Riky will like it. I don't wish anything more than Riky and Adi to be happy.

The wait of three years for our son was nothing in comparison to the wait between the plane landing at JFK and Riky finally getting out of customs. I marveled at how far we'd come in our journey, yet found ourselves in the same spot where Adi had waited for me to emerge from customs years before. Our emotions ran high and I felt as if my heart was beating so hard it might jump out of my chest. Would Riky even recognize us? What would he say? Millions of questions raced through my weary mind in a mix of joy and anxiety. I can still picture that little bundle of a human walking slowly next to our good friend, who did everything possible for us to be reunited with Riky, and had accompanied him on the journey. When they got close to us, I could see Riky trying to inch his way into hiding behind his companion. He wore the jacket we had sent to him. His hair was quite long, almost down to his shoulders, and his blue eyes seemed full of questions that, in his silence, he wasn't yet ready to ask.

Adi had reminded me not to run and hug him, not to overwhelm him. "We'll have to take it slowly," he'd said. "We are almost strangers to him. We'll need patience." A mother couldn't hug her own son. But he was right. I approached Riky gently, bending down and saying hello to him. He was shy, quiet, and tired.

On the car ride back to the apartment, I sat in the back seat with him. When we reached the apartment, we showed him his newly renovated and painted room, complete with a new bed and Flintstone sheets, a tiny couch, and a chair with an animal print. He looked around with curiosity, but tiredness took its toll. He didn't even want to eat.

"Can I go to sleep here?" he asked. "I am tired."

"Of course," I answered, and dared to give him a quick kiss before leaving him to rest. *I have time now*, I thought. Having him there with us was unreal. All other problems became either nonexistent or suddenly easy to concur. The biggest challenge of our lives was behind us.

It had been a long journey to bring Riky over, but we still had a long journey to restore our bond with him. We worked full time and I attended college full time. We had no relatives nearby and we couldn't afford a nanny. We found a preschool that was a bit far from us, but we liked it a lot and registered Riky there. After being in the US for only two weeks, we had to enroll Riky in the preschool full time. Though he didn't know English, he learned quickly and soon made friends, including one who would become his best friend. The other boy's mom still remembers how she went to pick up her son one day and found the two of them in a corner sharing a lollipop.

Between college, work, and home, I was overwhelmingly busy. Fortunately Adi's job allowed him to drop Riky off at school in the mornings and pick him up in the afternoons. They'd often go to the park for a bike ride or come visit me at work. Many times they would pick me up in Manhattan from work and drop me off in Brooklyn at college, and then at 9:00 p.m. they would pick me up from college to drive me home. After I transferred to Baruch College in Manhattan from the City Tech College, my commute by subway became manageable. In those days I was working six days a week. I'd wake early to be at my first class shortly after 7:00 a.m., then rush to work, after which I'd return to college for more classes. Most nights I didn't get home until very late. I took anywhere from four to six classes at a time. I wanted to get college over with so that I could get a good job and begin providing more for my family.

In the meantime, Adi shined in his engineering job. Our changing circumstances did nothing to diminish his amazing perspective and vision, which seemed to include anything at which he tried his hand. He was an incredible engineer and designer. He couldn't look at a piece of machinery or equipment without redesigning it and improving it. His brain itself was designed to design. He was adept at taking a problem and finding a solution for it. While he excelled at mechanics and electronics, he also had a deeper understanding than most of medicine, of politics, nearly any subject he chose to focus on. I started calling him my walking encyclopedia. He was very rarely wrong, but on those infrequent occasions, he was also the first to admit it.

Though Adi's skill as an engineer was apparent—he even went so far as to secure a patent—he also longed to return to the skies. Whenever he could, he'd visit a small airport on Long Island to log in flight time so that he could get his private pilot's license. I always knew that Adi's passion for flying would lead him back to that career even if it took him years to accomplish it. Whenever we were at an airport, Adi would say it smelled nice, though the only odor was that of gasoline fumes. It was at an airport or in the sky where Adi was as comfortable as he was at home. Flight was embedded in his soul.

Our difficult journey was equally difficult for our son. He was forced to quickly adapt and learn a new language. Not long after his arrival in the US, I became pregnant with our second son, during what was probably the busiest and craziest time of our lives. I was a full-time student, worked full time as a nurse's aide, and of course was a full-time mom to Riky. Adi did most of the parenting, laundry and household chores. My classes were scheduled either very early or very late, so that I could still work ten hours during the day. I felt I had superpowers and I did it all. My OB-GYN suggested using the natural birthing center since my pregnancy was going well and I wasn't at risk. I gladly accepted the idea. It was right across from the doctor's office at Roosevelt Hospital in midtown Manhattan.

When the contractions came one night around 11:00 p.m., we jumped in the car and drove from Queens to the hospital in Manhattan. The staff checked me in and confirmed the baby was coming, but they wouldn't open the birthing center and we couldn't understand why. They had me hooked up to various monitors in the maternity ward. The contractions continued, increasing in intensity. This time Adi was by my side, unlike Riky's birth in Romania, where men were restricted from the birthing rooms. He kept asking the nurse to call my doctor and move me to the birthing center, which was one floor down, but they kept delaying the move without giving a reason for it, or mumbling something along the lines of it not yet being time to "bother" the doctor. The contractions were coming stronger, but Adi told me that the indicators on the monitor weren't moving that much.

"I don't care what the monitor says," I pleaded, "it hurts!"

Adi scurried from the room to find a nurse and told her that the machine didn't seem to be working properly. As soon as she adjusted the monitor pads on my belly, the indicators sprang to life, jumping up and down on the monitor with such volatility that I felt the machine might break. Adi stared at the monitor dumbfounded and at a loss for words. At that point I began freeing all the tubes and suction cups from my belly.

"I am not supposed to be here to begin with," I said, disappointed. "Nor am I supposed to have anything on me." In that moment I wanted nothing more than to be free of all the equipment and left to deal with pain in my own way.

Adi trailed the nurse out the door, pleading with her that it was time to call the doctor, to which she finally agreed.

They moved me to another room without any visible equipment, just a simple bed and a desk. By the time the doctor came it was 4:00 a.m. He rushed into the room and asked me if I still wanted to go to the birthing center. At that point I didn't care. I felt the baby was almost ready to come into the world and the contractions were too intense and close to each other.

"Let's take her to the birthing center, please," Adi said on my behalf. "That's what she really wanted."

I was placed, with no small amount of pain, on a stretcher and taken to a private room in the birthing center on the floor below. The room looked like a nice hotel room. It held a bed, nightstand, dresser, paintings on the walls, and a big bathtub to ease the pain. I didn't get a chance to use the bathtub or rest once they put me into bed, however. I wanted to rest a bit, but the doctor's voice decreed, "You don't have time to rest. You've got to push! The baby is here." Three great efforts later and Andy was born at 5:00 a.m. with Adi by my side. It was the most wonderful feeling in the world.

The nightstand next to me had special sides that pulled up out of nowhere to form a small crib. The painting that was above it slid along the wall to reveal a hidden compartment stocked with newborn supplies. We had everything we needed and Andy never left the room. After I settled in and Andy fell sound asleep, Adi went home to get Riky. When my firstborn arrived, he marveled at the tiny creature called his brother, but his attention soon shifted to the bathtub. "Can I use it?" he asked. And he did. At least one person in the family was able to.

Our health insurance allowed me to stay in the hospital for forty-eight hours. That was the deal: no medication, no additional expenses, I got the nice private room but I couldn't stay more than forty-eight hours. On the afternoon of the day I'd given birth,

Adi looked at me and asked, "Would you be willing to go home tonight? Whatever we do here, we can do at home." I agreed and was discharged twelve hours after bringing Andy into the world on June 11, 1997.

* * *

In the summer of 1998 I graduated college and started my job in IT early the following year. Life was moving fast and at times getting in the way of restoring our bond with our firstborn. Emotionally, we were falling behind. Riky experienced more difficulties than a child should and, as a result, had to grow up faster than he was supposed to. Andy brought us great joy, but having a new baby also took away from our precious time with Riky, which hadn't been much to begin with. They grew fast and both boys needed more and more of our attention.

A few years later Riky and I were at the library where we encountered some of his classmates. The two brothers were there with their father. I said hello, but Riky remained silent. When we left the library, I asked Riky why he hadn't said anything. He didn't want to answer, but I insisted. Eventually, he whispered, "Because they pick on me."

Shocked and indignant, I took him by the hand and we rushed back into the library. We found the boys and their father, whom I told what I had just learned.

The father scolded his sons, reminding them how it felt when they'd been picked on in preschool. We left the library with the promise that the bullying would stop. My adrenaline was still racing when I later told Adi about what had happened. The experience opened our eyes to how difficult things must have been for Riky, not only adapting to a foreign country but also to his own parents.

At Riky's school we spoke with his teacher and then the school counselor. We told her our story. She listened quietly before telling us that because of our experiences, our bond with Riky had been broken. We needed to learn how to restore it and have a healthy parent/child relationship. We needed to be patient and it would require hard work. Adi and I were devastated. It was the first time in my life that I saw my husband cry and the first time that he regretted leaving Romania.

"If I'd known that my actions would take such a big toll on my own son, I never would have left," he whispered with a soft, broken voice.

Though Riky was bullied, traumatized by moving to a new country and having a little brother to compete with for attention, he was both smart and capable. The challenges of life taught him to focus and his inner strength helped him to do well later in life.

Nonetheless, at that moment our eyes were truly opened to the reality that we needed to slow down and amend what we had broken. It would take us years and it wouldn't be easy, but our relationships needed both healing and connection. In our rush to make a better life for our children, we inadvertently hurt them along the way. It was a choice no parent should face, between a lack of future or causing young children pain, but such was the position in which we found ourselves. We'd made our choice, working for the future, but in many ways we still needed to reconcile with the past.

21

GRIEF DIVIDED IS MADE LIGHTER

With our new lives established in America, I couldn't help but want the same for my loved ones. I spoke with Nelu about joining us in the United States. He was on the verge of agreeing, when everything changed on September 11th of 2001.

On that fateful day, I should have been under the twin towers, which was the last stop of the path train in downtown Manhattan that I took on my way to work. I was delayed that morning, registering Riky for a local chess club. By the time I reached the parking lot in Harrison, New Jersey, to get on the train, the first plane had already hit. A parking attendant told me not to go into the station. When I heard the dreadful news, instinctively I looked up, mesmerized by the beautiful clear day. I couldn't imagine such a thing happening and I went in anyway. By the time I got on the path train, the second plane had hit. My fellow commuters and I watched in horror as smoke enveloped the twin towers. The enormity of what we saw, even at a distance, left us dumbstruck. I thought about calling Adrian; he was flying that day. The cell phones stopped working.

The train stopped in Journal Square station, and within minutes there were hundreds of us, confused and worried people waiting on the platform to see which direction we would be heading. I waited for an hour, planning to go uptown first and then take a subway downtown to work, when I eventually gave up and took the return train home. I found Mamaia, who was with us at that time, in the middle of the living room in tears watching television, worried about what was happening and worried about me. A glimpse of smile washed over her face at the sight of me, followed by the command, "Call Adi right now, he is worried sick about you." At that moment the phone rang and it was Adi. He was ecstatic to hear I'd returned home safely. He'd received the news of the plane crashes while still flying himself, but had held off on telling the passengers to avoid panic. His plane was diverted and he landed in State College, Pennsylvania, originally having been bound for LaGuardia, New York. He was among the first ones to rent a car and just drive straight home, recognizing the gravity of the situation and the weeks of confusion that would follow, with no guarantee on when flying would resume.

Mamaia screamed.

With the phone still in my hand, I turned around to see the first tower collapse. And then the second. When Adi arrived home, we watched in pain and through tears the events that followed. Adi and I were together and safe.

Nelu never again entertained the possibility of relocating to America.

* * *

After leaving Romania, we had no hopes or desire of returning soon, as we were afraid that we might never again manage to leave. Eventually the time came to take up the challenge and return to the US embassy in Bucharest to get the visa stamped on our passport. We had approval for it, but at the time the only way to finalize the visa was to get a stamp at the US Embassy in our home country. We were both fearful for our return to Romania, but didn't have a choice. We needed that legal status of residency in order to move on with our lives. Adi decided to go alone first. Flying in, instead of enjoying his return to our country after so many years, he worried about the outcome. What if the visa was denied? How would he get back to Riky and me in America? Fortunately, his interview went well, the US Embassy granted him the visa, and he was able to return to us without incident.

A few months later, Riky and I had to make the same trip for the same purpose. After receiving the visa, we left Bucharest for Salonta to visit family. Once home, I found that Nelu was not himself. By that time he'd been sick for a few years without even knowing it. In time we'd learn that he'd contracted Hepatitis B. He wasn't sure of the source but suspected the dentist. In those days, dental tools were reused from patient to patient, and never fully sterilized to begin with. He'd been lethargic, often falling asleep in the evenings in front of the television. It happened once while I was there, and I remember Sorina looking at me with a mournful smile. "It happens a lot," she said. "He's just so tired."

The Hepatitis B diagnosis took a while, and by the time his symptoms were properly identified, his doctors told him that he had only a fifty percent chance of successful treatment. His health continued to decline. That visit was bittersweet. While I relished the opportunity to reconnect with my brother, the reality of his condition settled in upon all of us like an unshakeable chill, and I said goodbye to him at the end of that trip with a sadness in my heart.

My brother wasn't the only family member whose health had been failing. One cold January day, I got the call that my mom had passed away. Adi had been unable to attend his mother's funeral, as she'd died, at the tender age of forty-three, while we were in the States, without the proper paperwork that would allow us to come and go at will. Unlike Adi, who'd been unable to attend the funerals of both his mother and brother years before, I was able to go, so I readied myself to travel for the funeral while Adi stayed home with the kids.

I had mixed feelings about returning home again. I loved my mom. It hurt losing her even more in light of the fact that now both of my parents were gone. I wished we could have been closer.

Thinking back on the fact that she had Nelu and I so young, I couldn't help but see her as a kid having kids of her own.

My mom and dad were fifty-nine and forty-nine, respectively, at the time of their deaths. Adi's father still seemed healthy as he entered his sixties, the last of our parents and the only one who might make it to old age. Sadly, he too then passed away, at the age of sixty-three. Though he'd still been in good physical condition, he died by accidental electrocution while fishing. Adi and I were heartbroken to lose the last parent and it's very sad when I think that my own kids grew up without having grandparents, but what choice did they have?

My days home for my mother's funeral were heartbreaking and overwhelming, so much so that I seized joy where I could. When my uncle told me that my cousin was getting married that summer, something took my heart by storm and I immediately exclaimed, "Uncle, we are coming in the summer to the wedding! There is so much sadness around. I would like to come back for a happy event." And we did just that. That trip in the summer was amazing. For two weeks we drove around beautiful Romania with Nelu and his family. I bonded with my brother, remembering the old times and seeing Nelu like I always knew him, despite his declining health. We danced at the wedding, gliding across the floor in each other's arms, not realizing that it would be the last time we would do so. For us, right then, it was about floating around the dance floor, just as we had as teenagers and in our hearts we were teenagers again. All the years of being apart were forgotten, evaporating into thin air. If there was ever a reminiscence of the painful past it was all gone. I left him wondering how his health would progress and if I would see him again soon.

A year later, when I was back in the States, Nelu emailed me, telling me that he'd been informed by his doctors that only a liver transplant would save his life. He was forty-three years old. At the time, transplants in Romania were largely unheard of and Nelu didn't consider it a viable possibility. Even his doctors doubted whether or not it could be done with success, despite having just admitted that it was his only hope. I did my best to both plead with and educate Nelu on the fact that an organ transplant was not only possible, but could also succeed in saving his life. I was desperate and determined that my brother's life would not be cut short by the shortsightedness and limited capabilities of his medical staff. He listened and eventually agreed that he would pursue the liver transplant. I breathed sweet relief at the news that he was not simply giving up on his own survival.

This was in the summertime and by December he received word that an organ was ready for transplant and he was next in line. He called me on a Friday while I was commuting to Manhattan by bus. I wanted to fly to Romania at that moment, but he told me to wait, as they weren't yet sure whether the liver in question was a match. Regardless of his wishes for me to hold off, I jumped on the first flight to Bucharest that evening.

Relatives picked me up at the airport with the good news that not only was the liver a match, but Nelu had already undergone the surgery that morning and was doing well. They said his swelling was subsiding and the color of his face was an indication of returning health. I wasted no time in seeing him. My younger brothers Doru and Marius were there as well. We visited Nelu every day, laughing, reminiscing, and joking around, the four of us reunited.

It was a Tuesday when I visited and could sense the doctors were agitated. When we were alone, Nelu confided, "It was a close one, I think. I knew I was in trouble even if they didn't come out and say it." He saw the worry register on my face. "It's alright," he reassured me. "My body isn't rejecting the liver and I'll be fine. I'm going to make it. Besides, I need to live at least another ten years to see my kids get through college."

He smiled then and I relaxed a little as we talked about college for our children. Nelu wanted his son Andrei to become an engineer.

"I thought he wanted to be a doctor?" I said.

"Yes," Nelu conceded. "But I think he should do both. He could have engineering as a backup. It's what worked for me."

"Medicine is the type of career you put your full focus on," I said. "Let him become a doctor; he seems so passionate about it and focused to succeed."

"Maybe you're right," said my brother, giving in.

The following Saturday, a full week after the operation, Nelu was doing well and preparing to move out of the ICU the following day. We were all in his hospital room and I was saying my goodbyes, as I was to fly out the following morning. Nelu began complaining of feeling cold one minute, and hot the next. My brothers and I exchanged glances, sharing an unspoken suspicion that he was developing a fever. We summoned a nurse who put Nelu back on an IV. "I'll alert the doctor first thing in the morning," she said.

Our farewells extended until 10:00 p.m. that night. Doru and Marius said their goodbyes, as they had to leave as well. Once they'd left, I was alone with Nelu. I hugged him, my brother who was always cheerful and cracking jokes, but who suddenly turned serious.

"Please take care of Adi and the kids," Nelu instructed.

"I promise I will," I said. I kissed him and left with a heavy heart.

The next morning, Doru and Marius took me to the airport. The three of us decided to call Nelu before it was time to go. It was Nelu's birthday, December 13. He was turning forty-four years old that day and we knew he'd asked Sorina to bring pizza and soda to the hospital to share with the nurses and staff in celebration. But as we tried to reach our big brother, his cell phone just rang and rang. He never picked up and an uneasy feeling settled over us. We kept quiet. Painful thoughts crossed our minds, but we were too frightened to voice them to each other. My plane was leaving soon, so I kissed Doru and Marius goodbye and headed to the gate, looking back in hopes of a sudden phone call that would give me what my heart longed to hear.

My flight home encountered turbulence, something I was of course familiar with, but which had never bothered me before. It bothered me then, but I was also preoccupied with Nelu's well-being.

I arrived home on Sunday afternoon, and Adi was there to pick me up from the airport. Adi and Nelu had always been very close, and I knew that Adi loved my brother as much as I did. Only a day passed before Mamaia called that Monday. All she could say was, "Nelu is not with us anymore. You have to come back."

Tears came instantly. "How?" I asked. "What happened?"

"He went back in for surgery. He'd developed an infection and they tried to save him, but there was nothing they could do."

I told her I'd call her back, hung up the phone, and repeated her words to Adi. He looked at me in shock for a moment before he began pacing the dining room, alternately holding and shaking his head in disbelief.

"You told me he was doing well," Adi said. "The new liver was okay. I don't understand. How could he possibly just die like that?"

I wanted to get back on a plane that evening, but Adi was worried about my wellbeing.

"You are exhausted," he said. "Please don't go tonight. Get a good night's sleep and I'll book a ticket for you to go back tomorrow."

That night, emotionally drained, I collapsed into Adi's arms.

"The last thing he said to me was to take care of you and the kids," I said. "You think he knew?"

"I don't know. Maybe."

"When he had that emergency on Tuesday, when the doctors were worried, he knew," I said, giving voice to my suspicions. "He told me so."

The next day I flew back to Romania for the funeral. There was no time for mourning. Nelu's wife, kids, my brothers, everyone was hurting. I did my best to offer comfort, especially to Nelu's wife Sorina. I could not imagine the pain of a husband passing away at 44, leaving her with two children. I could not fathom what Andrei and Adelina felt, losing their father when they needed him the most. I dedicated myself with all my heart into supporting the family Nelu left behind, forgetting about my own needs and neglecting my own necessary grieving for my brother. It would surface weeks later, out of nowhere, while I was riding the bus home from work. Without warning, it hit me in a wave of sadness and tears poured down my face. I got off the bus a few stops early and just stood on the sidewalk, sobbing. I called Adi to come pick me up. He was alarmed at hearing me cry with abandon, but when I managed to utter the name "Nelu," he understood. He picked me up and drove around quietly for an hour so that I could regain my composure before we went back home to the kids. I didn't want to worry them with my pain and distress.

When I flew back home to America after Nelu's funeral, my plane again encountered turbulence, this time even more severe. I struggled to withstand both the turbulence and my brother's death. It was too much; I couldn't take any more shaking when what I needed was peace, and began to associate it with death. From that moment grew a fear of flying. It snuck up on me when I was most vulnerable and could only be calmed if I flew with Adi. With my husband by my side, I would cling to his arm and he'd reassure me. Whenever we flew together and encountered troubled skies, Adi would put his hand over mine and say, "It's very mild and nothing to worry about." And then I'd close my eyes and exhale in relief.

The culmination of my dear ones' deaths and funerals meant that most of our trips back to Romania, at least in those early years, were accompanied by clouds of sadness, which had inadvertently become intertwined with my love of the skies.

* * *

Though my unease of turbulence sometimes lingers, I get better with each flight. A while back when Riky was a student in Rochester, we flew many times to see him. One morning we woke to low visibility and I wasn't a fan of the sky that day, while Adi proclaimed enthusiastically: "The airport just opened. Let's go!"

Shortly after takeoff, the tower made contact: "A Cessna on the downwind reported it encountered clouds. Are you okay?"

"Yes," Adi replied. "I see a break in the clouds and I'm going for it."

But the higher we rose, the more clouds and fog seemed to envelop us. It was a game between Adi and the natural world, but one which brought me only discomfort.

I didn't want to take the controls and fly that day. I took pictures of the world below whenever the fog relented. It seemed to be improving; it was *supposed* to be improving. We were a little over 4,000 feet, crossing the Poconos towards Binghamton. But the weather forecast got it wrong. Terribly wrong. What was supposed to get better and clearer suddenly closed in on us. I could hardly see the ground. Clouds were under, around, and above us. The horizon grew narrower and my anxiety heightened.

"Let's go back home," I suggested. "This doesn't look right."

"Well, we can't go back," Adi said. "We hardly made it out of Caldwell and now it's even worse."

It was true. The airport we'd taken off from closed again after our takeoff.

"Then let's find another airport to land at," I said.

With Adi's thousands of hours of flight experience, he still believed we'd be fine. "The current conditions will hold for another twenty to thirty miles," he said.

The minutes that followed felt like infinity. I desperately wanted to safely land where we could see something in front of us—the horizon would have been nice. Finally, Adi spotted clearer skies and headed for them.

Flying has always been part of our lives. We bought our first small plane, a Skipper, years ago, and then later purchased a Liberty XL2. We put aside our dream of getting the plane we truly wanted, a Diamond DA40, until three years ago. I wanted my diamond and I finally got it! Taking to the skies—the ability to spread our wings together—is our passion.

We take trips whenever we can. We have our favorite, usual jaunts, like flying to New Haven, Connecticut to pick up pizza from Pepe's, then flying back home to share it with family and friends. Finding the hidden gem airports that are close to hiking or biking trails is another treasured pastime. We pack our foldable bikes, cycle around and get a meal before returning home. We make our own happiness. Together.

In time, flying together and sharing our passion, even those trips when we seemed mired in clouds, helped me overcome my fear of flying in turbulence. I can't imagine giving up flying. It's embedded in both of us. At the same time, flying helped me reconcile and deal with the pain of losing my brother. Often when we take to the skies, I think of Nelu. I asked him to help me make peace with my feelings and I let him know that, just like he asked me to, I kept my promise to take care of Adi and the kids. And I always will.

22

EVERY CLOUD HAS A SILVER LINING

Our lives moved to a fast cadence. We didn't know what the future held, but we liked to think that, come what may, we'd all be in it together. Most of the time, the good things that happen in our lives stay on the surface of our memories, and a fog settles on the hardships and struggles. The suffering of that time in our lives surfaced again when I dusted off an old letter to a friend, a letter I'd never mailed.

> *It was a very difficult time for us. After years of effort and running around, I finally finished college in the summer of 1998. After taking six courses in one semester while having a baby and a small child at home, getting only two hours of sleep at night and incurring a lot of debt, I was finally able to search for work.*

> *I had no idea how difficult it would be to get hired: small companies would have hired me but I had no experience, while big companies would have hired me but I had no green card. After a lot of searching and interviewing, I finally received two offers, one of which I accepted in October 1998. Since the new job began in February of 1999, I took a temporary position in the sales office of a watch factory to bring in some money.*

> *When I started a permanent job, I was in training for three months. I left for work in the mornings before the sun came up,*

and I'd arrive home at night after 9:00 p.m., sometimes as late as midnight. I was returning home exhausted. I'd bathe the kids (if I was home in time for it) and tuck them into bed. Andy slept in my bed and woke often during the night. The next day, I'd start it all over again. In that fall I lost weight suddenly, over thirty pounds in three weeks, and I was very weak and experiencing low blood pressure. I even lost my smile—any energy I had left was spent on taking care of my kids at the end of the day.

If I would have not been anemic and overwhelmingly busy, and not so stressed from starting a new job at a good company with no experience and worried if I would perform well, if I would have slept at least a night from evening to morning uninterrupted, if I would have...if I would have...probably I would have been a calm, normal person.
But I was like a zombie during that time, going through the motions of life. I am lucky that Adi had patience with me to get better.

I physically began to improve in the springtime; my soul grew calmer as well and found more peace. Our home was always full of love, but at that time was also very agitated. I was probably too ambitious that I tried hard to finish college sooner and I took a lot of courses while I worked full time and I got pregnant. Then I gave birth but the run continued. Nothing is free. Everything comes at a price. Did I have a choice though? We felt we did the right thing in what we did.

Adi and I love each other very much, just like we did in the beginning. He was always next to me for better and for worse. If it wasn't for his words of encouragement I don't know how I would have finished college with everything else going on.

He trusted me and helped me to discover my resourcefulness. I wanted to go for my master's degree but I have put it on hold since Adi got a job as a pilot. He put his entire career on hold for me to get mine going, and now is the time to focus on getting him back in the cockpit. Everything has its time and place. Family is more important right now.

Sometimes I wish I wasn't quite so giving and trusting, since many times this leads to disappointment. I can't change though. I like to help people and trust them even if I stumble sometimes. I hope that someone else will come and pick me up. And then I regain my trust that still there are true souls and not everything is lost.

* * *

To fulfill our dream and integrate better into society, we decided to move from Queens to the suburbs. We bought our first home, which needed a long list of improvements, in Livingston, New Jersey. It was an ambitious plan but one that became a reality in 2000. We wanted our kids to grow up like other American kids. We scraped together $11,000 for a down payment, a bit from our newly opened 401(k), some from our savings, and most of it borrowed off of credit cards. At the beginning, we barely survived our mortgage combined with the cost of living in Livingston.

Adi worked primarily as a mechanic, fixing coffee machines and other restaurant equipment, while simultaneously in pursuit of a job in engineering, which he managed to obtain. He continued to shine, in true Adi form. Though he didn't even drink coffee himself, he ended up designing the largest coffee machine there was at the time, one which produced 6,000 coffees in a single hour for a hospital in Canada. He even went on to secure a patent in conjunction with Lipton. Adi's invention made Lipton's tea thirty percent stronger, but with the same ingredients.

Despite his successes in the corporate world, I knew that Adi's spirit longed to return to the skies. When the opportunity finally came for Adi to resume his career as a pilot, we knew the shift would come with a drastic pay cut. Money was precious and scarce, and because of it, Adi had to balance his return to flight with continued engineering work during his hours on the ground. Trying to find the sweet spot between chasing your passion, providing for your family, and being present for your family was an elusive equation for both of us over the course of many years.

Every weekend was spent working on the house, cleaning up the roof, painting, altering the kitchen; the house was always being worked on. It needed a lot of repairs and we couldn't afford to hire anyone, so we worked hard, completing many improvement projects by ourselves.

We broke every financial rule in the book during that time, but we didn't have the luxury to wait or be less aggressive in our planning. Our first time around, we took the usual path like everyone else. Now, we were starting a second life and time was against us. We had no time. It was different. It was a rush to catch up, a rush that impacted our kids. I was a very strong person but there were so many tasks to carry! That first job after graduating college, working for GS, a financial company, was incredibly demanding. I loved my job, the people! But I lost so much being away from my family. Andy, when he was about four years old, took my Blackberry and threw it in the trash. "I hate GS!" he screamed. Those words still resonate with me.

Despite the turmoil, I will forever be grateful to the company and HR. While Adi's employer had been hesitant to sign off on our needed green card paperwork, GS was a great help and generous with its effort and compassion. They put my paperwork through, allowing it to be processed faster and making up for considerable lost time.

We couldn't afford to hire a babysitter and instead asked Nelu's mother-in-law Mamaia to help us. She did, leaving her family behind on more than one occasion to travel to the States and help us with the kids. She was like a grandma to our boys, a kind woman with a big smile on her face, and someone who loved our children dearly. After a few years Tataia, her husband, began joining her on those trips, as it was difficult for them to be apart.

After ten years I lost the GS job, and it was the best thing that ever happened to me and my family. I started cooking and dancing while cooking. Being happy. I learned to be really happy and bond with our boys. We settled down and money was no longer a strain. Riky was eighteen and soon heading off to college, while Andy was entering his teenage years.

Andy and Riky had been very different as children. Andy was a cheerful, happy child, but with sudden tantrums that we didn't think much of at that time. While he was little he made an impact on Riky, because the attention went to Andy. We didn't see Riky growing up. It was like we looked at Andy and saw Riky growing up too. The difficult years hit Andy towards the end of middle school and in high school. We couldn't understand the changes in him and we attributed them to the angst of teenage years. Later on, we understood that while he was bright, it was difficult for him to focus. He struggled to sit still and was easily distracted. Not much kept his attention, with a few exceptions like volunteering as an EMT, where the adrenaline ran high and he found joy.

When it was clear that Andy wasn't happy or content with himself, I struggled to understand what he was going through. His life experiences and environment were so different from those in which Adi and I grew up, so it was difficult to relate. Adi and I believed we did our best to let our children's personalities take shape on their own. Looking back, I think of what we could have done better. How might we have helped more and been more understanding? We did our best with the information at hand and in that situation. Our own toll took a toll on our kids. We did it for them and I hope they appreciate the effort and forgive us for our mistakes. Not understanding Andy's feelings and loneliness is one of my greatest regrets.

Our actions were in pursuit of better lives for our children, yet we were hurting them at the same time. Where is the balance? We eventually found it, but it took time. I made peace with myself when Andy one day told me that he recognized how Adi and I tried to not imprint our views on them. He acknowledged that we let them judge for themselves and only when they got older did we begin sharing our beliefs. It wasn't easy. Could we have done better? Yes, for the kids. But otherwise, better for whom and what? Each chose their own path and with a little luck, but mostly hard work, we got there, measuring success against our own values.

In all the craziness we must have done something right. On my last birthday, Andy gave me a letter:

> *It is hard to express in words how much you mean to me. I hope it is never questioned that my love for you has and always will be unconditional. Though I know we have had times in our lives where it has seemed like we were both at odds, I believe that it has only made our understanding of each other grow. I will never know how hard it is to be a mother. Through trials and tribulations, you've gritted your teeth and overcome so many obstacles to give Riky and me a chance to become successful and happy. It must have been impossible to see all the different outcomes when you first came to America, starting your life over not knowing what may lie ahead. I understand in my heart that every decision you and Dad made was with the intention of giving your children the opportunities you could have only dreamed of growing up in Romania.*
>
> *If I had to pick one word to describe you it would be "resilient." Though it may have been all too easy to give up at any step of*

the way, you pushed through. Though a backdrop of poverty and alcoholism made up the tapestry of your childhood, you refused to let yourself give into it. Though people mocked your dreams and tried to dissuade you at every turn, you would not allow it to deter you from the path you set out for yourself. I admire you so much for that. I could never imagine having to push through all the hardship, and luckily because of your efforts, I won't ever have to experience that. You have always been a role model for me; even now while I spend long nights studying I think of your story and I use it as motivation. I think of your resilience as I try to develop my own.

Thank you for everything you've given me. I will cherish it forever.

* * *

A few years ago, one morning Riky came to talk to me… specifically me. He seemed so serious. I just hoped nothing was wrong.

"Mom, do you like Florencia?" he asked.

"Yes, I like her. She seems nice," I answered.

"Mom, do you really really like her?" He repeated the question. I looked into his blue, kind eyes and I realized he was too serious for the morning hour. He wanted to know my honest opinion. He was twenty-four years old; he knew he didn't need my approval to date a girl. Why suddenly? Why this girl? Was she special to him? For a second it crossed my mind that in the end that's all that matters and that's our successful parenting: when we don't interfere much but they know the family values and find them valuable. He wasn't seeking my approval but he wanted to make sure our values were still the same. I was proud.

"Yes, I really really like her," I assured him. "The only thing I'll tell you is we fought hard for our green card. Don't take it lightly."

"Mom, that's not the case if we get there. All her family is in Argentina and from what I gather from her she would never leave them. My challenge would be if she wants to leave everything for me, to come here."

Where had I heard that before? Does history repeat itself? I wished my own son wouldn't have to go through immigration pains all over again, but if he met the right girl for him, it's worth fighting for. He married his sweetheart three years ago.

* * *

What kept me sane through tumultuous times? Adi and flying are inseparable. The skies still unite us and give us peace and an inner tie and beauty that's hard to explain. Up there it's just us and the rest of the world is down there, somewhere, forgotten along with all worries. I've always wondered at the meaning of happiness and think that it varies from person to person. For me, happiness is being content with myself, understanding that I can't please everyone, as well as the importance of picking my battles. Intrinsic to happiness is love. Adi and I have now been together for thirty-seven years. He had a trip to Florida on our anniversary, so without hesitation I hopped on a plane to be with him. We didn't require any lavish plans for our anniversary, strolling on a beach or visiting airfields is good enough for us, because the importance lies only in being in one another's presence. Our bond keeps us going and dreaming of what's ahead. We don't know what the future holds, but we do know that we'll experience it together.

23

BETTER LATE THAN NEVER

When my father died, the last hope of having the house finished died with him, like clouds erased from a windswept sky. I was away in Constanta starting a new life, revelling in the joy of a promising future with my husband. Nelu was in Oradea starting a new life as well. It would have been difficult to help with anything, as we were each beginning down a path of creating our own families. Nelu, being closer, always tried to help our mom and brothers as best he could. He struggled to say "no" to Mom's requests, whether or not it was in his own best interests.

After our dad passed and his military unit closed down in Oradea, Nelu moved to Salonta to be even closer to Mom, putting a toll on his own family by doing so. Oradea was a bigger city with different possibilities for his family, or he could have gone to Bucharest to be closer to Sorina's family. He could have been transferred, I am sure, to nicer cities, but he chose not to. In the end, when his military unit closed in Salonta, he decided, finally, to move to Bucharest, where they would be close to Mamaia and Tataia, Sorina's parents. Overall, it was a blessing. I just wished he would have done it sooner, or moved closer to me in the States, as by the time of his Bucharest move, I'd already emigrated.

It was before moving to Bucharest that he was diagnosed with hepatitis B. Maybe if he'd taken more chances, his life would have been different and I would have my big brother now.

Marius never left home, even after he married. It was customary for a child to remain in the parents' home, not only as someone to pass the house onto, but also so that the next generation would be there to care for the parents as they age. Marius fathered twins, a boy and a girl, with his wife Gina. Their family of four lived in the main house while my mother moved to the smaller second house. He started drinking more, illustrating that history repeats itself. I could just imagine how Gina raised those two little babies mostly by herself. I could relate to her struggle and what it's like to deal with the decline of someone you love, as I'd been in a similar situation with my dad, but for Gina it must have been harder since she had to support two small kids and her income wasn't much, and when Marius wasn't working, his income was nonexistent. I don't know how she managed. In the meantime, their kids were growing and the house was falling to ruins. Whatever was there, whatever Dad managed to build, was falling brick by brick. The kitchen became unusable and Gina moved the kitchen into one of the two other rooms. This left all four of them sleeping in one room that was also used as the living and family room. The main hallway, used as a sitting room next to the kitchen where Mom had a couch and small stove, was falling apart as well. Mold crept up and into the walls, pieces of plaster, drywall, and ceiling regularly fell down. Doors began to rot.

 The small hallway at the entrance of the home, Gina managed to save. The other house, where Mom lived towards the end of her life, was also falling apart and served only the purpose of storing wood for the winter, and occasionally letting the dog stay there in the harsh winter days. When I visited my parents' house, instead of seeing what Dad built to be saved or continued to be worked on, it was quite the opposite. It was very depressing. It was like I wanted to run away from the painful past and the painful present. At one point Marius fell very sick and was told that he had to make drastic changes if he wanted to live. Something clicked inside him and he found the strength to stop drinking and later on smoking as well. I hope he had a good marriage and life before all his troubles started, because when he got better, other news broke in to further take a toll on their happiness: Gina found out she had breast cancer...quite advanced.

While my brother navigated these trials, my family life continued to improve. Our jobs were more stabilized, kids were teenagers and we were in a better position financially. Little by little, all of my father's dreams of finishing the house became my dreams, working their way into my heart as surely as they'd been in his. I would not build multiple stories, but I would build a bathroom, a full kitchen, a third bedroom, and redo what was already built. It needed a full renovation. When my dad took the first build plans from the city, the house was a ranch. But then he couldn't finish it and it was left like that for years...He needed a new permit and by then the rules changed and he needed—in fact was obligated—to keep it as one story. Years passed and again he needed a new permit, this time one that allowed for two stories. We used to say that the second level was Nelu's and third was mine. I used to imagine myself sitting on a balcony with a clear view of the street, gardens, and beautiful open skies. Of course, despite the permits and best of intentions, nothing ever materialized beyond those two rooms, kitchen, sitting room and hallway.

I have no resentment over Marius living in the house for years without improving upon it. He might have thought about it when he got married, but once he started drifting, from both his health and life itself, money was scarce and the house was the last thing on his mind. Despite my lack of resentment, the unfinished state of the home still hurt me deeply, because I felt it had contributed to my dad's failed health. He dedicated his life to providing for us and making sure we were safe. It was just one element in a series of dashed dreams that culminated in his death. Doru would have had a better chance at making headway on the home, but he moved to a small apartment when he got married to Claudia. While he cared deeply about our parents' house, he had his own family and little daughter to worry about. I never asked why he decided to move and why Marius was left to live in our parents' house.

Adi knew about my dad's dream and that I'd never stopped thinking about it. When I brought the idea of a renovation up to him, he said that I should do what I thought was best. He knew how important it was for me to finish my dad's house and fulfill his lifelong dream. Even though Dad never showed preferences between his kids, I was the only daughter and there was a strong tie between us that I can't explain. In many ways, I am like him. When he was drunk and wanted to talk to me about his dream he would always start with, "Didica." It was his nickname for me when he'd had a few drinks and he'd let his guard down to show me his love.

Getting Adi's support in those times, especially when it wasn't cheap to finish the house, was just further evidence of our strong relationship and understanding. Even though throughout the process I shared the plans, the struggles, and how much effort it was taking, Adi never questioned anything. In our relationship it was normal for us each to fulfill our dreams if it was possible. Adi agreeing with me to finish my dad's dream and spending a lot of funds to make it happen was exceptionally kind of him, and a clear marker of the nature of our relationship.

While making the renovations, Gina grew sicker and sicker. I happened to be home one Easter when we were almost done with the construction. The kitchen cabinets were recently installed and Marius asked Gina to come and see them. She looked at us with tired eyes and fatigue from the chemotherapy and cancer running through her tiny body.

"Maybe tomorrow I'll go and see it," she said in a soft voice. The kitchen was only a few steps from where she was, but still miles away for her. "I'll feel better tomorrow." With dragging feet, she made her way to bed and collapsed slowly with a quiet sigh.

She was so kind; she didn't dare to make a noise, lest she extend her pain to us.

I invited a few cousins and my aunt Nani for Easter dinner that year. It was a warm day and we set the dining table up outside. We hauled an armchair out into the sunshine and Marius and I carried Gina to it. We fixed her a plate of food which remained largely untouched. She sat in the sun for the better part of the afternoon, surrounded by family. Though her body was wracked with pain, her eyes shone with happiness.

When the last item of furniture was in the house, Gina sadly passed away. I mourned not only her life cut short, but also that she was never able to enjoy the completed house and raise her children in the home she deserved. Instead, life taught my little brother how to take care of his children the hard way. At only thirteen years of age, they lost their mother.

When I visited the home after all the renovations were complete, I regretted that my father was no longer around to see it. I can imagine him looking at the house with inquisitive eyes and admiration, his weathered hands resting snugly at his hips, and nodding in approval. Would he have appreciated the way I changed the design plans, the hallways to the new kitchen, the relocated bathroom, the layout of the three bedrooms? With my eyes closed, I can catch a glimpse of his hidden smile of approval. After all, I was my dad's little girl. I wish I could let him know that his dream had been realized, forty-two years after he'd laid the foundation, but also twenty-five years after I'd had to give him my last goodbye.

In her years as a widow, my mother had also expressed regret that the house wasn't restored to my dad's wishes. In a way, finishing the house was in her honor, too. I like to think that she would have loved it very much and that, as well, she would have told me so. Looking back now, with my coffee in one hand and my thoughts in the other, I dream. My eyes are wide open. I look around in the garden, visualizing the projects and wishes. Then it strikes me: I am still Daddy's girl.

24

LOVE LASTS A LIFETIME

An Open Letter to My Adi…

In the labyrinths of life with intriguing challenges coming our way, we navigate by holding hands. If one falls, the other holds on tight, so tight that the spirit never breaks and finds the power to lift up. It goes higher and higher absorbing an immensity of energy. It builds up until we are stepping together again. If one falls, the other half finds the power to be a savior and lift the weight and step strongly ahead. We always find the supernatural strength to lift the other half up and forget our own limitations of being just human. For us, the other is the important one: no games, no selfishness. And by building the other one up, we always grow stronger together. I say, without a doubt, that our relationship is stronger than ever.

You are my other half and I am yours. We know each other in and out and we still discover new things about each other every day. We listen to our needs and deeply care for each other. We left our comfort zone so many times to reach out that our own comfort became being with each other every time, all the time. You are my darling and just mine. I am your darling and just yours.

Our pictures along the years tell a story of two souls embedded and tangled so deeply that it would take the world beyond a lifetime to untangle them: you hold me tightly or I hold you tightly. In every picture. Your eyes are smiling as you gallantly look at me as if you've just fallen in love with me and you are never willing to let me go. They tell the story of our journey together, our resilience and triumphs, our failures and accomplishments. Our hands touch, as if we've just fallen in love with each other. And we just did, again. For us, every sight of each other is as if we just fell in love for the first time. Your smile makes my heart melt, still does.

I sometimes affably say that you are obsessed with me. I admit that I am obsessed with you. The other day I told you that I want us to live forever to share what we have forever, that my worry is that one day we won't have this. I dread the day one of us won't. Those fears have no worth, as we live our lives every day as if it is the last day. We suffer every day we are apart and are truly happy when we're reunited. We find happiness in the smallest things: the sound of a cricket or bird, the rush of flight, the gurgle of a running river, or just sitting next to each other.

Many feel that we are lucky to have each other. We make our own luck; we've built this relationship and we work hard at it every day. They tell me that I am lucky to have you. That you are special and a rare find. That you would do anything for me, sacrificing your own well-being for mine. I hear but don't listen, it doesn't resonate with my feelings. For me, your care is natural and I appreciate it every single day. I do the same for you.

You find ways of giving me strength and bring out the best in me. I like myself when I am with you. And if someone ever can hurt you that would be only me. Sometimes I ask myself if I deserve you or what on earth could possibly make you fall in love with me and stick with me for so many years. You say it's ME: my good heart and my beauty of soul and kindness that many people fail to see. The way I love you and take care of you. The way I provide and never fail to improve and listen. The way I listen to you. The way I stand up for our boys. The ways I love them and dedicate myself to them. You once said that I am a gentle person, but I become a lioness when I need to protect our kids.

You spoil me and I spoil you. You listen with your heart. Life is harsh too many times and it hurts often. Holding hands and hearts we cruise through, amending each other's wounds and healing faster and better than ever. We are emerging on top, smiling and laughing.

We neither are perfect but we are perfect for each other. We would heartily say that the secret of our everlasting relationship is give and take…one of us can't keep on taking since soon enough there won't be anything left to take, just an irreplaceable void. The other will try to fill it back only to discover it became a bottomless well, but our balance of give and take is fostered by our mutual love and respect. We fill it and the void dissipates.

After so many years, I still find myself with your thoughts on my mind or repeating them like they are mine. It never crossed my mind if it's right or wrong to do so. Are the unified thoughts of two souls wrong? We think alike so much that we don't know who said what anymore.

It's an indescribable inner beauty to grow old with you. A day alone with you is a day in heaven, right here in reach on earth. I tremble when I know you are about to reach home and miss you already even if you haven't left yet. Our home is our paradise.

We never forget we have each other. As time goes on, love deepens and evolves. It's the worry when you don't call, the care when you ask me if I am hungry, the chivalrous look in your eyes when you tell me that you "love me enough" when I ask you if you love me.

"Why enough?" I ask.

And you answer with nonchalance: "You want me to say a lot? What if a lot is not enough? My love for you, it's endless, and I'll always have enough love for you and I give everything I have to you."

Adi has always instinctively known when to be by my side, show me his love and support, and when to step back so that I might stand on my own. This balance, his ability to love me endlessly, to have enough love for me, to love me without obsession, without suffocating me, is a gift. It is an amazing and rare gift to love me, simply, enough. And to love me just enough provides a cornerstone for my own strength and the very bedrock for our everlasting relationship. I will treasure it forever.

***

It's like a circle. I wish to find myself and I do when I see you. It gets difficult when you are not home or you leave for a few days or a week. The longer I do not see you the more I do not recognize myself and the longer it takes me to find myself...to grasp all the pieces and put them together.

Yes, I panic when you leave for a long time. You take me with you and I have to find myself from so little, from small pieces scattered all over. Without you it would be more difficult and take much longer to get myself together—to be myself again. Chances are that I would never collect all the pieces...and that would be fine since some of them are yours to begin with. You've given them to me. You've completed me. I've always wanted to thank you for that...and for being you, for loving ME...I've never found the words.

ENOUGH LOVE

First year cadets with our flight instructors before parachuting for the first time.

Waiting to onboard the plane for my first jump with a parachute.

Running to Adi with the excitement of completing my first flight solo.

Harsh winters during Air Force College didn't stop us being together.

Adi on airdrome before flight.

With our IAR-316B helicopter flight instructors.

Adi getting ready to fly IAR-823 airplane.

Adi ready for flight mission in L-29 Delfin military jet trainer.

Getting ready to fly IAR-823 airplane.

Military parade.

Training in Air Force College on IAR-316B Helicopter.

Graduation from Air Force College as Lieutenant.

ENOUGH LOVE

Civil Ceremony: in our Air Force Dress Uniform.

Civil Ceremony: in our Air Force Dress Uniform.

Made in United States
North Haven, CT
31 May 2023